A Talmud Tale

A musical from Rabbi Judith Abrams
Book by David Schechter and Ned Paul Ginsburg
Lyrics by David Schechter
Music and Additional Lyrics by Ned Paul Ginsburg

Teaneck, New Jersey

A TALMUD TALE (A MUSICAL) ©2004 Ned Paul Ginsburg and David Schechter. All rights reserved. No part of this book may be used or reproduced in any manner whatsoever without written permission except in the case of brief quotations embodied in critical articles and reviews.

CAUTION: Professionals and amateurs are hereby warned that A TALMUD TALE (A MUSICAL) is subject to a royalty. It is fully protected under the copyright laws of the United States of America, and of all countries covered by the International Copyright Union. All rights, including professional, amateur, motion picture, public reading, television, video or sound taping are strictly reserved.

Published by Ben Yehuda Press
430 Kensington Road
Teaneck, NJ 07666

A Talmud Tale is a project of Maqom: A School for Adult Talmud Study, supported by grants from The Covenant Foundation, The Houston Jewish Community Foundation of the Jewish Federation of Greater Houston and many other generous donors and foundations whose names can be found at http://TalmudTale.BenYehudaPress.com/donors.html.

To license a performance of A Talmud Tale (A Musical), please visit http://TalmudTale.BenYehudaPress.com or contact Maqom (*maqom@compassnet.com*,) (713) 723-2918. For licensing for professional productions in which the majority of the proposed cast would be members of Actors Equity, please contact the authors at ned@nylamusic.com.

Library of Congress Cataloging-in-Publication Data

Ginsburg, Ned.
[Talmud tale. Libretto]
  A Talmud tale : a musical from Rabbi Judith Abrams / book by David Schechter and Ned Paul Ginsburg ; lyrics by David Schechter ; music and additional lyrics by Ned Paul Ginsburg.
    p. cm.
ISBN 978-1-934730-28-7
  1. Musicals--Librettos. I. Schechter, David, 1956- lyr II. Abrams, Judith Z. III. Title.
ML50.G494T3 2009
782.1'40268--dc22
                    2009033752

For more information about A Talmud Tale, including details on acquiring the musical score, music for the songs, and clips from the play's premiere production, please visit http://TalmudTale.BenYehudaPress.com

A Talmud Tale (A Musical) was first produced at the Jewish Community Center of Houston in February, 2007.

Producer's Preface
by Judith Z. Abrams

"Shivkuha! Sheli, v'shelachem—shela hu!"

Said Rabbi Akiba to his followers: Leave Rakhel alone, for my Torah learning and your Torah learning are due to her. (B. Ketubot 63a)

Who can learn Torah with joy? Anyone can! Especially when they have the support of their spouse. The quote, above, is said by Rabbi Akiba to his wife, Rakhel, telling all the world that it was she alone who saw that he could become a great sage and sent him off so that he could learn Torah.

This musical is meant to be a continuation of Rakhel and Rabbi Akiba's commitment to a joyful and engaging was of learning Talmud so that everyone feels comfortable. After all, Rabbi Akiba did not know the aleph-bet when he began his studies. So truly, anyone, no matter what their background, can learn Talmud with joy.

A musical seemed to be just the right vehicle for teaching these texts: requiring practice and repetition to achieve memorization and then bringing words on a page to life. Those engaged in Torah and Talmud study are privileged enough to do this every time they open a holy book. Rabbinic literature, of which Talmud is the major work, is full of enough magic, love stories, perilous journeys, wars, tears, miracles, sacrifices and triumphs to keep any theater in scripts for decades. So this is just a beginning in what I hope will be a mission of musicals based on Jewish texts. (As Rabbi Tarfon says: You are not called upon to complete the work but you are not free to abandon the work—M. Pirkei Avot 2:21.)

This musical touches on modern themes (e.g., parent-child conflict, ridiculously overdone celebrations when children reach maturity, rigid standards of "success" that reveal parents who see their children as extensions of themselves rather than as independent individuals[1]). Then

---

[1] These problems are rife in our community and deserve examination within the context of Torah study. When a parent can write the following words, you can see we are in trouble. One father writes, "My children notched terrific [SAT] scores, but I would love them even if they hadn't. The question is: would I love them as much? The answer, sadly, is no. Though it pains me to admit it as a parent, having children who got high SAT scores makes ordinary social interaction easier. You don't have to rationalize, tergiversate, dissemble or sneak

it shows how these issues existed thousands of years ago and how our ancient texts can help us navigate our own life's trials. In this musical, we meet them: our eternal support group. These ancient friends show us how to live honestly and faithfully, love romantically and passionately and listen to that still small voice inside us rather than to the loud chorus of voices that tells each of us, 'You can't!" Instead, our ancient friends sing out, "Anyone Can!"

This musical was designed to be an entertaining and educational way to introduce learners to the Talmud. From the start, I envisioned it being used by synagogues, Jewish Community Centers, Hillels, Jewish camps, youth groups, Jewish day schools and community performing groups. The script and score are accompanied with educational materials about the characters and stories referred to in the musical. These passages of rabbinic literature can be found at Maqom's web page *http://talmudtale. BenYehudaPress.com/sources.html* These passages, accompanied with explanations and discussion questions, can be used as a curriculum and then the show could be performed as a summary project of the course. These educational materials could also be used by performers who want to know more of the background of their character's life.

Two versions of the show (long and short) have been developed. Both versions need only keyboard accompaniment although woodwind parts and guitar chords are included as well and greatly enrich the music. The show can be staged with very few performers or as many as you'd like. Adaptations to accommodate performers whose voices have not yet changed are also available in the score. (See the Composer's Preface for more detailed information.)

The musical's book is by David Schechter and Ned Paul Ginsburg, lyrics by David Schechter, with music and additional lyrics by Ned Paul Ginsburg. I know you will enjoy their brilliant work. I want to thank them and all the performers and audience members who helped us shape the show into the script you presently hold. I want to thank my own family for their support and patience and to express my thanks to God for all that has been given to me.

This project is supported by grants from The Covenant Foundation, The Houston Jewish Community Foundation of the Jewish Federation of Greater Houston and many other generous donors and foundations who are listed at http://www.maqom.com/musical.html. Without their out of the room when the subject is broached. (Joe Queenan p. 242, *Town & Country Magazine*, November 2004.)

support, this project could not have been achieved. I am grateful for their generosity, not only of money but of faith, as well, in as far-reaching (and, as it must have seemed, far-fetched) a project as this one. Jeff Dine and others worked long hours to bring this show to you. I am deeply grateful for their generosity and devotion. For more information about this project, contact Rabbi Judith Z. Abrams, Ph.D., Founder and Director of Maqom at *maqom@compassnet.com*.

Judith Z. Abrams

Author's Preface
by David Schechter

A musical is like a page of Talmud. It can be interpreted many different ways. One can pick out a variety of themes to emphasize. What is told can be taken as literal or metaphorical or both. Characters may be perceived as symbols or as actual living, breathing beings.

Like a page of Talmud, our musical, A TALMUD TALE, exists in several different historical periods simultaneously. First there is the modern layer, peopled by the bat mitzvah girl, Rachel, her rabbi, her family and friends. Their cultural perspective would be closest to ours, as present day students of Jewish tradition. Rachel's opening song, "So Many Questions," strives to give comic voice to the ambivalent struggle between the sacred and the secular in our modern Jewish world.

The next layer is ushered in by Rashi and Shlomo, both visitors from the Middle Ages. They serve as guides and bridges between the modern and the ancient worlds, much as the commentaries of Rashi (which hail from the twelfth century) do on an actual page of Talmud. This historic figure and his companions woo Rachel into the past with a song comparing "An Open Book" to a door into other realms of learning.

Finally, the show leads us back to the First Century, C.E., the period of Jewish study and religious debate that existed right after the destruction of the Second Temple, a time of profound Jewish scholarship that gave rise to the Talmud in the first place. There we meet the fabled Rabbi Akiba, a shepherd until the age of forty, his beloved Rakhel, the legendary Rabbi Eliezer and many others.

The historical multi layeredness of A TALMUD TALE is intended to reflect the patchwork quilt of perspectives one finds in the Talmud itself, where opinions of rabbis from different centuries sit side by side on any given page.

Just as the stories and directives on a page of Talmud may be followed to the literal letter or interpreted metaphorically, so the production style of A TALMUD TALE may be historically specific and literal or as expressionistically abstract as the director and designers choose. Akiba's flock of sheep, for example, may be represented as anything from a group of small kids (merrily bleating) to projected film or slides of an actual flock, to the pantomimed apparitions of a skilled actor playing Akiba, accompanied by recorded or live sounds. I personally tend to be of the "less is more" school of theatrical design. Since the show shifts frequently from present to past and from place to place, I am inclined to suggest that a few simple props or pieces of furniture aided, if possible, by an inventive lighting design, can accomplish a lot with a little. But if the resources and desire are there, one could create a more elaborately designed representation of Akiba and Rakhel's ancient world and of Rachel's abundantly materialistic present day reality.

THE TALMUD TALE can even work quite effectively as a sort of staged cantata, with all of the performers onstage and visible at all times, seated until they are called upon to enact a scene. This approach emphasizes the ritual nature of the event, connecting it in yet another way to the religious traditions it speaks about.

The show is written to be performed either by a cast of actors whose ages are appropriate to those of the characters or by a cast of imaginative younger performers in an educational environment. It is our hope that whoever performs it will feel their humanness enriched and their Jewishness deepened by putting on the robes, figuratively and literally, of this passionate and colorful array of characters, soaking up their history from the inside out, meeting them, as they themselves sing, "Halfway" between the present and the past.

I would be remiss to end this author's preface without offering my heartfelt thanks to my co-librettist, the composer of THE TALMUD TALE, Ned Paul Ginsburg, whose discipline and creative gifts are of the highest order. And to Rabbi Judith Z. Abrams for inviting me to dive into the deep world of Talmud in the first place, where she enthusiastically and tirelessly guided me and Ned toward the wealth of theatrical characters who live there. It was Rabbi Abrams who first had the wild and wise notion that we might find a way to express the voices of this soulful and ancient Jewish crew in song.

Judith Z. Abrams

Composer's Preface
by Ned Paul Ginsburg

The score of A TALMUD TALE is an amalgam of styles representing multiple influences in my life: American musical theater, jazz, Ashkenazi (Yiddish) folk music, and Sephardic music heard while I was a teenager living in Israel. Some musical choices came completely intuitively, others were made with a conscious effort to be inclusive of the wide sphere of music that the Jewish people have taken part in over the centuries.

This piano/vocal score is provided with a woodwind line and chords for guitarists. Some words of explanation may be helpful here:

Vocal lines/tempi:
The vocal lines have been notated in different clefs, depending on the range of the singer and the number of singers in a given song. This is SATB writing, for the most part. Occasionally I have provided lower, "optional" notes in melodies which are rangey. Transpositions of solos and duets are certainly possible. I have chosen to use tempo descriptions instead of specific metronome markings, trusting that musical directors will find tempi that work for the ensembles they are leading. Swing rhythms, such as in "The Perfect Mother," have been notated in simple eighth notes, with the understanding that the first eighth note gets two-thirds of the beat and the second eighth one-third. Dynamics are indicated, where necessary, above the staff.

The piano part:
The piano music is intended to be playable on its own, meaning, without woodwinds or guitar. There is a fair amount of melody doubling, and also, doubling of the woodwind lines. However, it was not possible to double every woodwind line in the piano part. Obviously if a woodwind artist is available (see below) the music becomes richer and more satisfying. I have chosen to leave out pedal markings since in my experience pianists tend to have an innate sense of where and when to use the sustain pedal.

The woodwind part:
In staged readings that were part of our developmental process, a woodwind doubler was employed who played flute, clarinet and alto sax.

There is roughly an equal amount of flute and clarinet music. If local communities cannot find a suitable doubler it is certainly possible to use separate flute and clarinet players. I would not recommend having a flutist play clarinet music or a clarinetist play flute music. The alto sax is used in only two or three of the loudest songs, and it is possible (though not preferable) to replace the sax part with clarinet.

The guitar chords:

The guitar chords provided are intended for solo guitarists who are providing accompaniment for piano-less productions. There is a frequent use of extensions: 9ths, 11ths, 13ths, and suspended chords. A chord with a slash followed by a letter of the alphabet means "play that chord over a particular bass note." To the extent that any guitarist can capture these harmonic features and subtleties, he/she should do so. Some harmonies may be simplified; a capo may be helpful on some songs.

Underscores:

There are a number of underscores in addition to the sung songs of the score. These are provided in some cases with repeats or safety vamps to cover unknown amounts of transition time between scenes.

Ned Paul Ginsburg, composer

New York City, 2004

Judith Z. Abrams

Cast of Characters
(in order of appearance)

From the present:

RACHEL COHEN, 13 years old
RABBI LIPPMAN, her rabbi
ELAINE COHEN, Rachel's mother
STUART COHEN, Rachel's younger brother
SARAH, Rachel's school friend

From the past:

RASHI, a medieval Jewish scholar
SHLOMO, his scribe
AKIBA, a shepherd, 40 years old
RAKHEL, a wellborn Jewish woman in her early 20's
A ROMAN SOLDIER
BEN KALBA SAVUA, Rakhel's father
RABBI ELIEZER, famous head of a study house (Beit Midrash)
MEIR, a Jewish student
MARTA, a wealthy Jewish woman
BEN DAVID, Ben Kalba Savua's "lieutenant"
ANCIENT ENSEMBLE (playing assorted roles)

TIME:
  Now and approximately 60-130 C.E.

PLACE:
  13-year-old Rachel's modern world and ancient Jerusalem

List of Musical Numbers

ACT ONE:
1. "Overture"... Orchestra
2. "So Many Questions"....................... Rachel, Mother, Friend, Brother
3. "An Open Book"................................ Rashi, Shlomo
4. "Welcome To The Talmud".................. Ancient Ensemble
5. "I Am Not Myself Today".................... Rakhel
6. "Up To You"....................................... Akiba, Ensemble
7. "Who Are You?"................................. Rakhel, Akiba
8. "Not Another Man"............................ Rakhel
9. "A Crown Of Straw"........................... Akiba, Rakhel
10. "Both Sides Of An Issue".................. Rabbi Eliezer, Akiba
11. "Am I Right?"................................... Mother, Ben Kalba Savua, Rachel, Rashi, Shlomo
12. "What Does It Mean?"...................... Rabbi Eliezer, Akiba, Rachel, Rashi
13. "So Many Questions (Reprise)"......... Rachel
14. "Welcome To The Talmud (Reprise)". Ancient Ensemble

ACT TWO:
15. "Entr'acte"...................................... Orchestra
16. "The Perfect Mother"....................... Rachel, Mother, Brother, Friend
17. "An Open Book (Reprise)"................ Rashi
18. "Anyone Can".................................. Akiba, Meir
19. "Not Another Man (Reprise)"   Rakhel
20. "Old As Time"................................. Rashi, Ancient Ensemble
21. "Both Sides Of An Issue (Reprise)"... Rabbi Eliezer, Akiba
22. "Up To You (Reprise)"...................... Rabbi Akiba
23. "A Simple Shawl"............................. Rabbi Akiba, Meir, Others
24. "Anyone Can (Reprise)".................... Rabbi Akiba, Ensemble
25. "Halfway"....................................... Ben Kalba Savua, Rakhel, Rachel, Mother
26. "Welcome To The Talmud (Finale)"... Rachel, Ensemble
27. "Curtain Call /Anyone Can (Reprise)" The Company

A Talmud Tale

ACT ONE

(Spotlight on RACHEL, a 13-year-old girl. SHE is agitatedly fiddling with the buttons on a small tape recorder, trying to locate a particular spot on the tape.)

RACHEL: Okay. Let's try this again.

(SHE hits the play button and we hear the RABBI begin to chant the Torah portion "Vayeitsei (Genesis 28:10-16)." RACHEL haltingly sings along, going over a section again and again. SHE finally stops the tape and screams in frustration.)

Aargh!

(Lights up on RABBI, a middle-aged man or woman. HE/SHE is warm and genuine, but also overloaded with details and somewhat distracted.)

RABBI: Go easy!

RACHEL: I'll never get it.

RABBI: Of course you will.

RACHEL: I won't.

RABBI: There's still plenty of time.

RACHEL: 43 days?!

RABBI: (figuring, checking) Hmm. November 10th?

RACHEL: Yes, November 10th. That's exactly 43 days from today!

RABBI: And God made the world in seven!

RACHEL: Well, let Him try a bat mitzvah! (catching herself) ... Sorry.

RABBI: Look, everyone goes through this. Why don't we take a break?

> (The RABBI gestures towards RACHEL.
> SHE hands over the tape recorder.)

Now, how's your speech coming along?

> (RACHEL looks up in distress, then
> shows the RABBI an empty pad of paper.)

RACHEL: Nada! Blank! Nowhere!

RABBI: Rachel! You're making it harder than it is. Just ask yourself: "What does this Torah portion mean to me?"

RACHEL: But Rabbi, I don't even know where to start!

RABBI: With the text! Right there in plain English.

RACHEL: It's Hebrew.

RABBI: Oh!

> (hands her a book of translations, opening
> it to the right spot)

Here. Translation.

RACHEL: (despairing) It's like trying to explain poetry!

RABBI: Exactly! Just read between the lines. I'll be back.

(Exits. RACHEL heaves a sigh and begins to read aloud.)

RACHEL: "With a stone for a pillow, Jacob lay on the ground. And he had a dream.

(MUSIC under.)

He dreamed of a ladder reaching all the way up to heaven, with a stream of angels climbing up one side and down the other. And a heavenly voice promised to stand by Jacob always. When he awoke he sat up and said: 'Surely God was in this place and I, I did not know!'

(SHE slowly rereads the last statement.)

'Surely God was in this place....and I....I did not know.'....'I did not know'....'I did not know'...."

I don't know either!! People have been studying these words for centuries and I'm supposed to come up with something new?

RABBI: (poking head in) Rachel, don't sweat it so much! Relax. Let your mind go! Let yourself dream...just like Jacob!

RACHEL: OK, fine. I'll let myself dream. Here I am ... I'm dreaming....I'm dreaming....

(RABBI disappears again. RACHEL sings.)

[Song: " SO MANY QUESTIONS"]

I'm dreaming of the day when it's over
I'm dreaming of a way to survive
I'm dreaming, like Jacob, a ladder will appear
To get me out of here alive

I'm dreaming of a month in Aruba
But I'm sentenced to a year in jail
The rabbi says to read between the lines I see
But it might as well be in braille

And there are so many questions
I don't know where to begin
Who's there about
Who can help me out
Of this biblical maze I'm in?

So many questions
And all I can do is cry
Maybe I'll get lucky
And die

(MOTHER appears, in "to do" mode)

MOTHER: Rachel, are you sure you don't like that Laura Ashley dress? You don't really want to wear pants, do you?

RACHEL: I like pants. There are dress pants.

MOTHER: You're a Bat, Sweetheart, not a Bar.

RACHEL: Well, Duh!

MOTHER: You know how darling you look in pink!
    (Coaxingly)
And you would match the invitations!

(SHE reaches into a box and enticingly pulls out a pile of elaborate pink invites.)

RACHEL: I don't want to match the invitations.

MOTHER: Color coordination can be very impactful!

RACHEL: Mom, why are you stressing so much about what I'm gonna wear?

MOTHER: I just want everything to be perfect. This whole thing means a lot to me. And time is running!

RACHEL: Tell me about it!

MOTHER: We have a lot of choices to make…
          (takes out a list, ticking off items)
We still have to choose the band, the centerpiece, the yarmulkes…

RACHEL:
    There's so many things to be "chosen"
    Is that how the Jews got that name?
    Will friends say: "How clever,
    How charming and how chic!"
    Or will they wish they never came?!

MOTHER:
    I've narrowed it to sushi or primerib
    But I'm stuck on chocolate mousse or flan
    The caterer is coming at eleven ten
    And the florist is due at one

    And there are so many questions

RACHEL: (overlapping)
    Such pointless questions

MOTHER:
    So many things to decide!

RACHEL:
    I need a tack
    To get off track
    Of this roller coaster ride!

(Her younger brother STUART and her school friend SARAH appear)

STUART: Yo, Sis! You pick the theme?

RACHEL: The theme?

STUART and SARAH: For the party!

SARAH: How about MTV?

STUART: Or "Survivor!?"

SARAH: Or…. "Barbie's Dream Bat Mitzvah!"

RACHEL: Why does a bat mitzvah need a theme?

STUART and SARAH:
    So many questions!

MOTHER:
    From menus to…

    (RACHEL joins in mockingly)

    "…What to wear."

MOTHER:
    Please, at least, pretend
    That you care!

RACHEL:
    I care….

MOTHER: (to herself)
    You'd never know it
    From the way you behave

RACHEL:
    I do....

MOTHER: (to herself)
    Care to show it?
    I'm your mom, not your slave

RACHEL:
    I'm trying my best like you!

MOTHER: (overlapping, to herself)
    "Trying's" a good word for you!

RACHEL:
    I wish...

MOTHER: Where's your list of invites?

RACHEL:
    You knew....

MOTHER: We don't want anyone to miss your special day!

RACHEL:
    That I've got questions too!

MOTHER: You know, when I was your age, most girls didn't even have bat mitzvahs. I certainly didn't. My father didn't think it was important. Oh, bar mitzvahs, sure! Both my brothers had them. But, not me. Why should his daughter be honored?! So, don't go taking all this for granted!

    (The following all overlap.)

STUART: I know this awesome DJ! Want me to call him?

SARAH: I heard this girl actually had 'N Sync at her party!

MOTHER: Now, when the florist comes, he's going to want a decision. Roses or freesia?

RACHEL: Do you think maybe Jacob didn't know it was a dream at all?

MOTHER: Are you even listening to me?!

RACHEL:
    So many questions!

ALL except RACHEL: (singing in counterpoint)
    So many questions

RACHEL:
    With no one to show me the way
    I'm on my knees
    Won't somebody, please,
    Clue me in on what I should say?

ALL except RACHEL:
    So many questions!

STUART and SARAH:
    The music

MOTHER:
    The food

MOTHER, STUART and SARAH:
    The hall

RACHEL
    But if those are all the questions
    Then it leaves me with one question:
    Should I even get bat mitzvah'd...

        (RABBI reappears, carrying a big box of books)

RABBI: Rachel, have you made any headway?

RACHEL:
    At all?!

> (RACHEL scribbles a big sad face on her pad, holds it up and lets out a despairing scream.)

Ahhhhh!!!!

[End of song.]

> (MOTHER, STUART and SARAH vanish. RABBI starts unpacking the box of books.)

RABBI: Rachel, calm down.

RACHEL: (almost in tears) I feel like Kate Winslet on the Titanic and all the life boats have left!

RABBI: Here. This may save you. We just got this spanking new set for our library...

> (HE hands her one of the books he is unpacking)

...and you will be the first beneficiary!

RACHEL: (reading the title) "THE TALMUD, WITH COMMENTARY BY RAY-SHEE"?

RABBI: (correcting her pronunciation) "Rashi." It's kind of a nickname. For a great rabbi. From the eleventh century! He wrote to help people like you and me.
    (RACHEL looks at the book suspiciously.)
I'll check back.

(HE takes off again.)

RACHEL (calling after him) And what's "The Talmud?" (feels the weight) Another book! Why even open it?

    (SHE opens the book reluctantly. A magical musical chord strikes.)

RASHI: (offstage, a cappella)
    So many questions!

    (RASHI, an energetic man, enters busily, trailed by SHLOMO, his assistant, who is fastidiously scribbling on a note pad. The following dialogue is delivered in rapid-fire pace:)

RACHEL: Wha—?

RASHI: —Oh, a shayna maidle!

    (to SHLOMO)

Don't write that. But so long in the face! Okay, down to business!

    (RASHI and SHLOMO approach RACHEL.)

Who—?

RASHI: —Questions later! First, the preliminaries!

SHLOMO: (reading from a checklist as HE writes RASHI's answers) Hair?

RASHI: Brown.[*]

---

[*] These can be changed to suit the actress.

SHLOMO: **Eyes?**

RASHI: **Blue.**

RACHEL: **Blue-gray!**

SHLOMO: **Height?**

RASHI: **Same as my own daughter on her thirteenth birthday.**

RACHEL: **Don't ask my weight.**

SHLOMO: **Demeanor?**

RASHI: **(gleefully) Ooh! The demeanor question!**

    (stares RACHEL down, then drums a bit.)

Despondent, Category Four!

RACHEL: **Now wait—**

SHLOMO: **—We're almost done.**

RASHI: **Yes my dear, in a minute you'll come to understand the meaning of life!**

SHLOMO: **He exaggerates.**

RACHEL: **Oh, phooey!**

SHLOMO: **Page you're reading?**

RACHEL: **Page?**

RASHI: **The book, the page you're on...?**

RACHEL: Oh, I've barely opened it.

SHLOMO: The first page.

> (Done with his checklist.)

RASHI: A beginner!

RACHEL: I'm not a beginner! I've been at this sort of thing for months!

RASHI: Oh, but my dear, there are few books as unique, not to mention, as revealing, as thought-provoking as, "The Talmud, with Commentary by Rashi!"

RACHEL: You must be Rashi.

RASHI: She's smart.

SHLOMO: Intuitive.

RASHI: Shlomo, my scribe.

SHLOMO: I put down what I hear. No more, no less.

RACHEL: So, like, can I ask questions now?

RASHI: Fire away.

RACHEL: Okay, may I show you the door?

RASHI: Oh no, no, no. We're here to help you. You said you needed help.

RACHEL: Yes but—

RASHI: —Five minutes ago you were practically in tears.

RACHEL: (finally losing her defenses) Yes, but, how do you know that?

[Song: "AN OPEN BOOK"]

RASHI:
>Let's just say I'm good at reading things
>There isn't very much that escapes my eye
>From a mile away, you were clearly needing things
>And I can give you what you need, if you'll let me try

RACHEL: Try if you want. But it's hopeless.

RASHI:
>Even the hopeless can keep hopin'
>As long as they stay open

>>(HE opens the Talmud in RACHEL's hands to an inside page.)

Don't judge it by its cover.

>An open book
>Is like a door
>To take you places that you've never been before
>It's like a recipe for ev'ry dish you'd love to cook
>That's what it is—
>An open book

>You may feel stuck
>Or out of place
>Feel that a frown's the sole expression on your face
>Still there's a remedy to absolutely change that look
>And here it is:
>An open book

>(referring to the Talmud in RACHEL's hands:)

>Tales of adventure so involving
>You'll leave your worries far behind

Secrets told, myst'ries for solving,
Kick your feet up, unwind!

An open mind
An open heart
There can't be any better way for you to start
And we are here to persevere until you
Finish off the task you undertook
By hook or crook
There's help in the land
And it's in your hand:
An open book!

        (MUSIC continues under.)

RACHEL: That's very sweet, Mr. Rashi, but, how can I "finish" what I can't seem to begin?

RASHI: Oh, but you have begun.

RACHEL: (showing her pad) It's blank.

RASHI: You have pen, paper, and you have thoughts.

RACHEL: Yes, I'm thinking about crawling into a hole!

        (RASHI looks at SHLOMO for a brief
        moment. The ruse is "on".)

RASHI: She's slipping into Category Five!

SHLOMO: A tragedy!

        (HE pretends to pack up.)

RACHEL: Wait! What's Category Five?

RASHI: (rapid-fire now, as earlier) Pessimists!

SHLOMO: Victims of Self-Pity,

RASHI: Miscellaneous—

RASHI & SHLOMO: —Lost Causes.

RASHI: We haven't had a Lost Cause since?

SHLOMO: 1608.

RASHI: Yes, she was a stubborn one. Lost her mind.

SHLOMO: (making a "guillotine" motion) Lost her head.

RASHI: The loss was staggering.

SHLOMO: It left us—

RASHI: —not to mention her—

RASHI & SHLOMO: —speechless!

   (MUSIC out.)

RACHEL: I-I-I can change.

   (Pause.)

RASHI: Oh?

SHLOMO: Oh?
   (MUSIC.)

RASHI:
  Ohhh...Open your eyes to what's inside you

You'll be surprised by all you see
Though you long for someone to hide you
You got someone like me!

Your time is now
No turning back
And all the signs would indicate you've got the knack
But if you lose your way, I'm here to stay
And pester you until you're off the hook
Call me a shnook!
There's magic around
All because you've found
An open book

SHLOMO:
    An open book

RASHI:
    An open book

SHLOMO:
    An open book

RASHI:
    An open book

SHLOMO:
    An open book

RASHI:
    An open book

SHLOMO:
    An open book

BOTH:
    An open book!

[End of song.]

RASHI: Well? Still want to show us the door?

RACHEL: You can stay.

RASHI: Good.

RACHEL: But not too long, I have a—

RACHEL, RASHI & SHLOMO: —speech to write.

RASHI: Yes, the proverbial speech! Lucky you, not so long ago, girls never even gave speeches!

SHLOMO: (initiating a competition) Or had bat mitzvahs.

RASHI: Or voted for president.

SHLOMO: Or wore jeans!

RASHI: Or—

RACHEL: —Stop! I get the point. You're trying to make me feel guilty.

RASHI: Yes, so that you might lighten up!

SHLOMO: Live a little.

RACHEL: It's hard to "lighten up" when your mother is—

RASHI: (pulling her aside) —Rachel, we'll get to your mother, later. Now, let's focus on the speech. To express yourself—in speech—means you've arrived at certain conclusions.

RACHEL: Yes, yes, but I only have questions!

RASHI: Exactly. (pointing to the book in her hand) The Talmud is a place where all your questions are welcome. It's like a beautiful land—of words and stories.

SHLOMO: Of arguments,

RASHI: And solutions. A whole community of contrasting voices.

SHLOMO: Some harmonious. Some dissonant.

RASHI: But all singing, "Welcome!"

>(A gong is sounded. OTHER ANCIENTS appear.)

OTHER ANCIENTS: Welcome!

RASHI: Welcome, Rachel. To the Talmud!

RACHEL: (an uncomfortable realization) Is this the party?

[Song: "WELCOME TO THE TALMUD!"]

>(During the song, the ANCIENTS are shepherded around by RASHI, as they come forward to present different "books".)

SOLO MALE ANCIENT:
>The Mishnah is the base
>A very holy place
>It looks you in the face
>And tells you this is so

>It's the rock on which to stand
>A place on which to land

A Talmud Tale

> It helps you understand
> The laws you need to know

ALL ANCIENTS:
> But choruses are not all bass
> There's other voices, too
> That join in the chorale
> Of what it means to be a Jew...

RASHI: (referring to the Mishnah in her hands) It makes glorious music, as you can hear.

RACHEL: My grandma says I have a nice voice.

RASHI: Every voice is special.

ANCIENTS:
> So, welcome to the Talmud
> Welcome to our choir
> We come to enlighten,
> Inform and inspire
>
> Welcome to the Talmud
> It's a magical tome
> Oh welcome, and please
> Consider it home

RASHI: Just like you, the Mishnah has companions.

> (HE hands RACHEL another volume.)

FEMALE ANCIENTS:
> Embellishing a theme,
> Gemara joins the team,
> Connecting almost seamlessly
> To Mishnah's song

MALE ANCIENTS:
>While Mishnah sets the tone
>Gemara grinds the stone
>Puts meat upon the bone
>To leave you full and strong

ALL ANCIENTS:
>The two together become one
>And Talmud is its name
>Embrace it with your heart
>And you won't ever feel the same

RACHEL: (referring to the volumes in her hand) So, this is powerful stuff, huh?

RASHI: Not many books like it.

SHLOMO: And he's read 'em all.

ANCIENTS:
>Welcome to the Talmud
>Welcome to our choir
>We come to enlighten,
>Inform and inspire
>
>Welcome to the Talmud
>It's a magical tome
>Oh welcome, and please
>Consider it home

RACHEL: (looking in one of the volumes) These pages look so strange. I can't make heads or tails...

MALE ANCIENTS:
>It isn't left to right
>It isn't up and down
>Read the Talmud in circles

> Around and around

FEMALE ANCIENTS (in counterpoint with MALE ANCIENTS)
> It isn't left to right
> It isn't up and down
> Read the Talmud in circles
> Around and around

ALL **including** RASHI:
> So many voices
> So many points of view
> So much rhyme and reason
> So much study to do

SOLO FEMALE ANCIENT
> So won't you join the song?

SOLO MALE ANCIENT
> And won't you join the dance?

ALL
> We have so much to offer you
> So take the chance
>
> Oh, welcome to the Talmud
> Welcome to our choir
> We come to enlighten,
> Inform and inspire
>
> Welcome to the Talmud
> It's a magical tome
> Oh welcome, and please
> Consider it home.
>
> [End of song.]

RACHEL: That was really awesome. Thanks.

ALL ANCIENTS: You're welcome.

> (RASHI gestures to ALL ANCIENTS to be seated. THEY sit.)

RACHEL: But, how does this Talmud thing relate to me?

RASHI: Ah, good question. Shlomo!

> (SHLOMO takes note.)

We have parent/child drama, a struggle for independence, the search for meaning...

SHLOMO: You could go with the story of Rachel.

RASHI: Perfect!

> (RASHI gestures to the ANCIENTS to move to their "next position.")

RACHEL: Wait! I'm in there?!

RASHI: No, dear. Another Rachel. From long ago. Let's use her Hebrew name, "Rakhel." (Pronunciation: rah KHEL) Come, gather your things.

RACHEL: Where are we going?

RASHI: Only to Jerusalem.
> (He exits.)

RACHEL: Wait, I'm not even dressed!
> (SHLOMO shuffles Rachel off.)

> (Magical time-travel MUSIC. The year is 63 C.E. AKIBA, a shepherd, appears over a

hill outside Jerusalem. A man in his forties, he is rough and weathered, but attractive. SOUND EFFECT: the bleating of a flock of sheep. The sheep are mimed. In some productions, directors may choose to have small children play sheep.)

AKIBA: Complain all you want, it won't make the grass grow. Come on! Trust me, we'll find a better spot.

(Using his crook, HE ushers his flock across the stage. Before disappearing, HE notices one stray lamb.)

Don't daydream, little one, or you'll be left behind!

(HE ushers the little one off and exits. Enter Downstage RASHI followed by RACHEL and SHLOMO. RASHI is surveying the surroundings. RACHEL has put on a lovely robe from ancient times.)

RACHEL: I can't believe how well this fits!

SHLOMO: My father was a tailor.

RASHI: Okay, let's seat ourselves here. Remember, you can't talk to anyone. Not yet.

(To SHLOMO)

Details!   (SHLOMO writes.)

Outskirts of the city, 5 p.m. Things look a bit deserted. Rachel, at this point in time, around 60 C.E., the Romans controlled the land that in your day you call Israel.

(RAKHEL, the well-dressed daughter from one of the wealthiest Jewish families in Jerusalem, runs on. SHE is in an agitated state.)

[Song: "I AM NOT MYSELF TODAY!"]

RACHEL: **Is she a Roman?**

RASHI: **No! She is a Jew. Let's listen.**

RAKHEL:

Ah—
Ah—
How could I have talked back to my father?
How could I have thought he'd understand?
How could I expect he'd let his daughter
Get completely out of hand?
Usually I'm daughterly and docile,
Learning to accept my father's way
How could I have stamped my foot and shouted:
"I will not do what you say!"?
I am not myself today! Ah—

First there was a rabbi's son named Eli
Followed by the tall one, name of Zvi
Always from a family of importance
Yet that matters not to me!
Did my father think it would be easy,
Trying to arrange a "perfect match"?
Still, I really oughtn't to have cried out:
"I'm a woman, not a catch!"
I am not myself today! Ah—

Today, I am reckless and wild
Beguiled by the power I hold

A Talmud Tale

Today, I'm no longer a child
And I won't be bought and sold
Oh————
AH—————————

Probably he's wond'ring where I've run to
Probably they're searching for me now
Probably I ought to say, "I'm sorry"
But I'm not at all, somehow
And if they should find me on this hillside,
Telling me I've got some nerve to stray
When they ask me why my father's daughter
Thinks that she can act this way
I'll say:
"I forgot myself
But I am not myself!"
No, I am not myself today!
Ah————————

[End of song.]

> (RAKHEL remains transfixed in thought.
> RACHEL gets up and takes a step towards
> her.)

RASHI: Where are you going?

RACHEL: I want to meet her.

RASHI: You can't.

RABBI: Why not?

RASHI: You can't freely interact with anyone you choose! Please, come sit.

RACHEL: (absorbed in RAKHEL's aura) I know how she feels. You know, if my father tried to fix me up with some stupid guy, I swear, I'd stand up to him.

> (A ROMAN SOLDIER, impressive and intimidating, appears suddenly.)

Oh-my-God-I-think-I'll-sit.

> (SHE sits back down.)

SHLOMO: Good move.

RACHEL: Did her father send him after her?

RASHI: No, no! This one works for Caesar.

> (HE motions Rachel to keep quiet. The SOLDIER eyes RAKHEL and approaches her.)

ROMAN SOLDIER: Woman, you know it's dangerous to go walking unescorted.

RAKHEL: Oh, I know these hills well, Soldier. This is my father's land.

ROMAN SOLDIER: And who might he be?

RAKHEL: Ben Kalba Savua.

ROMAN SOLDIER: A Jew?

> (pause)

RAKHEL: Yes.

ROMAN SOLDIER: I see Jews are as careless with their daughters as they are careful with their money.

> (AKIBA, the shepherd, reappears over the

hill. HE stops a little ways away to observe
   the scene.)

RAKHEL: My father is not careless. It is I who choose to find solitude outside the city walls.

   (The ROMAN SOLDIER comes closer to
   RAKHEL)

ROMAN SOLDIER: (suggestively) Maybe you've found something better than solitude.

RAKHEL: (backing away) I don't know what you mean.

   (The SOLDIER advances and takes her by
   the arm.)

ROMAN SOLDIER: Oh, I think you do.

   (AKIBA rapidly moves in.)

[Song: "UP TO YOU!"]

AKIBA:
   Let her be!
   I could best you
   I'm a strong man
   And I know you've got an army
   You could beckon to a hundred men to fight
   But a hundred thousand soldiers
   Are a puny way to challenge what is right

ROMAN SOLDIER: No lowly shepherd tells me what to do! I am a Roman soldier!

AKIBA:
   Yes, and every move you make

Every action that you take
Makes a ripple in the waters of creation
And that ripple starts a wave
Though you hide out in a cave
You'll be flooded with divine retaliation

Up to you
It is always up to you
What you say
And what you do
Is up to you

Wisely choose
Will you gain
Or will you lose?
Can you put yourself
In someone else's shoes?
It's up to you!

> (THE SOLDIER releases RAKHEL and moves toward AKIBA, drawing his sword. CHORAL VOICES continue the song, under.)

ROMAN SOLDIER: You take your life in your hands, Shepherd, when you talk to me like that.

AKIBA: My life is always in my hands. As is your life in yours. What we each choose to do with it is what makes us who we are.

ROMAN SOLDIER: That makes you a dead fool any minute.

AKIBA: And you a blind one.

> (HE sings, joining the CHORUS behind him.)

> Because every move you make
> Every action that you take
> Makes a ripple in the waters of creation
> And that ripple starts a wave
> Though you hide out in a cave
> You'll be flooded with divine retaliation

If you do not treat her as you would want your own sister treated, then you do not understand what it means to be a man!

> Wisely choose!
> Will you gain
> Or will you lose?
> Can you put yourself
> In someone else's shoes?
> It's up to you!

[End of song.]

> (THE SOLDIER is still for a moment.
> Then, HE puts his sword away.)

ROMAN SOLDIER: I'll let you go this time. But only because a shepherd and a Jewess are hardly worth my sweat.

> (He turns to RAKHEL)

I'd advise you to guard your modesty more carefully.

> (HE leaves. RAKHEL turns to AKIBA, awed by what HE has just pulled off. Modern RACHEL turns to RASHI. The ANCIENTS do not hear them.)

RACHEL: **That was incredible!**

RASHI: **Indeed!**

AKIBA: (mischievously) It seems sometimes being "lowly" is an advantage! Goodbye, Miss. (HE starts to leave.)

RAKHEL: **Wait!**
(HE does.)

[Song: "WHO ARE YOU?"]

Who are you
That can wrestle a man down
Without touching him?

Who are you
That can weave a web of words,
Catch the truth and then present it
Like a sabbath meal?

Who are you
Wandering alone?

AKIBA:

I have never been alone
With the mountains and the sky
And my flock all standing by

RAKHEL:

Who are you?

AKIBA:

I am no one,
No one special,
Just a shepherd
Named Akiba.

RAKHEL:

Just an angel

AKIBA:
> Just a man

BOTH
> Just a man

AKIBA: And now that you are safe and sound, I hope you'll forgive me, but I must return to my flock. They too need my attention.

RAKHEL: (trying to keep him longer) The sheep are yours?

AKIBA: Oh no. They belong to a wealthy man in Jerusalem. Ben Kalba Savua.

RAKHEL: **My father!**

AKIBA: **Really!** All the more reason for me to get back to work! I hope you'll not tell him that I left them unattended.

RAKHEL: What I'll tell him is how you saved his daughter. I'm sure he'll want to reward you.

AKIBA: Your kind attention has been reward enough. I only did what any man would do. And now, I wish you well, Miss.

RAKHEL: **Rakhel.**
> (SHE offers her hand. HE hesitates. Then takes it.)

AKIBA: **Rakhel.**
> (HE smiles.)

Goodbye, Rakhel.

RAKHEL: **Goodbye...**
> (HE turns and goes.)
...Akiba.

Who are you?
Were you heaven-sent to me
To enable me to fin'lly find my destiny?
Or was I, perhaps,
Sent to help find yours?
Who are you?
Who are we?

>(MUSIC continues under. RAKHEL wanders off, deeply stirred.)

RACHEL: Oh, I get what's going on here!

RASHI: No doubt you do.

RACHEL: But isn't she like, way younger than him?

SHLOMO: By twenty years.

RACHEL: My mom says relationships like that never last.

>(SHLOMO scribbles.)

RASHI: And you agree?

RACHEL: (Pause.) I think it depends.

RASHI: On?

RACHEL: If they love each other—

RASHI: —Love?!
>(HE chuckles. SHLOMO scribbles passionately.)

And how do you recognize True Love?

RACHEL: I dunno. You just do.

RASHI: And what of Akiba and Rakhel? Are they— in love?

RACHEL: (as if in denial) No! They just met!

> (SHLOMO smiles and shakes his head as he continues to write. AKIBA and RAKHEL reappear together. There is a clear flirtation between them. RASHI and RACHEL can see them during this next passage:)

RASHI: And if I told you that since that day, Akiba and Rakhel have been meeting secretly every day for thirty days, maybe just for an hour, sometimes two, talking, discussing, trading intimate thoughts, even arguing?

RACHEL: I'd say, if they're arguing, anything's possible.

RASHI: (with sudden urgency) Oh! I think Rakhel has something important to say to Akiba. Let's— shh!

> (MUSIC out.)

RAKHEL: I have decided to stop resisting my father, and agree to be wed.

> (AKIBA is stopped in his tracks, surprised by his own emotion.)

AKIBA: (collecting himself) And who is the lucky groom to be? I'm sure a woman of your class has the pick of the crop.

RAKHEL: Yes, I do. And I have chosen the most precious fruit.

AKIBA: Are you sure he's the right one?

(MUSIC in)

RAKHEL: Oh yes. Quite sure. There is no one else remotely like him.

AKIBA: No one?

[Song: "NOT ANOTHER MAN"]

RAKHEL:

>Not another man
>As fair and humble as he
>Not another man
>As strong, but gentle with me
>
>Not another soul have I encountered half as kind
>He's the sort who'd stop to hold a needy hand
>When most pass blindly
>
>Not another man
>Whose vision cuts like a knife
>He's the only man
>Whom I would trust with my life
>
>Tell me I'm romantic
>As I tell you true
>Not another man will do
>Not another man but—

AKIBA: (interrupting) —You must feel relieved to have chosen someone! To find a man worthy of you, Rakhel, is no mean feat. He must be a wealthy man for your father to approve.

RAKHEL: Did I say my father approved?

>Not another man
>Who wears a sack like a robe
>Not another man

Who has the patience of Job

Never have I seen a generosity so rare
If this man were down to but a morsel
He would share it, gladly

Many other men
Have sold my father their worth
Promising a life
With every comfort on earth

But ask my father's daughter
Which of them will do
Is it any wonder who
Not another man but—

AKIBA: (interrupting again) —You can't be serious, Rakhel! How will you live, with a man who wears a sack? And sometimes is down to but a crumb of food?

RAKHEL: I will live like a queen. Because a crumb, shared with a good man, is more filling than a banquet shared with fools.

Tell me I'm romantic
As I tell you true

Not another man will do
Not another man but you

>   (AKIBA basks for a moment in what she
>   has said. Then a cloud crosses his face.)

AKIBA: Rakhel…your father will never allow—

RAKHEL: (hushing him)

—Not another man but you!

[End of song.]

(RAKHEL and AKIBA exit, eyes transfixed on each other. RASHI and SHLOMO stare RACHEL down.)

RACHEL: Why are you looking at me like that?...Okay, she loves him!

RASHI: But does he love her?

(Pause.)

RACHEL: He hasn't said very much.

RASHI: We usually don't.

SHLOMO: Speak for yourself.

(Pause. RASHI starts to go.)

RACHEL: Uh, I think Akiba's in shock. Hey, where are you going?

RASHI: Come. If we don't move quickly we'll miss the fun.

(HE exits. RACHEL follows SHLOMO.)

RACHEL: (with anticipation) Another love scene?

SHLOMO: Not exactly. Rakhel has something she must tell another man whom she also loves.

(HE exits.)

RACHEL: Another man?!

(SHE exits.)

A Talmud Tale

(RAKHEL'S father, BEN KALBA SAVUA, enters, followed by RAKHEL. HE is wearing glorious robes and dripping in gold jewelry.)

KALBA SAVUA: Well, you have my attention.

RAKHEL: Thank you, Father.

KALBA SAVUA: Well? (SHE hesitates.) What is it, Rakhel? Speak up.

RAKHEL: It's a subject dear to your heart. And one I know I've been very uncooperative about.

KALBA SAVUA: You mean marriage!

RAKHEL: Yes Father, I know I've seemed stubborn…but I have changed my mind.

KALBA SAVUA: Well, this is a blessed day. And none too soon, considering your age. I must say, it hasn't been pleasant feeling I'd have to force you to wed.

RAKHEL: Well, it was never marriage itself I objected to, Father. I knew once I met the right man—

KALBA SAVUA: So, Abuya's son Elisha pleased you after all!

RAKHEL: No Father, not him.

KALBA SAVUA: Then it must be Nakdimon ben Gurion's son. He too is a wise choice. And one I would be proud to—

RAKHEL: —His name is Akiba.

KALBA SAVUA: What do you mean?

RAKHEL: The man I will marry.

KALBA SAVUA: Akiba?

RAKHEL: Yes. He is in your employ, Father.

KALBA SAVUA: I know of no such man. What does he do, this Akiba?

RAKHEL: He tends your sheep.

KALBA SAVUA: This is a joke.

RAKHEL : No, Father.

KALBA SAVUA: (confused) A shepherd...?

RAKHEL: I'm certain you'd like him. Just last month, he saved me from a soldier in the road. You should have seen how he cut the Roman right down to size. And he never even touched him!

KALBA SAVUA: You want to marry an ignorant shepherd? And one who makes trouble with the Romans, no less?! Have you completely lost your senses?

RAKHEL: You have to meet him!

KALBA SAVUA: I don't want to hear another word about him. The son-in-law I pick will have the resources to provide a fine home for my grandchildren. And their mother.

RAKHEL: But he has a great soul.

KALBA SAVUA: Don't talk to me about souls! I forbid you to see this shepherd again. And I assure you I'll have him banned from my lands, as well.

RAKHEL: You don't even know him. If you'd just take the time to—

KALBA SAVUA: ENOUGH! The subject is closed.

> (There is a tense silence.)

RAKHEL: Father, I am going to marry him... with or without your blessing. But I'd much rather it be with.

KALBA SAVUA: You marry him, and as God is my witness, I will no longer have a daughter.

> (HE turns and leaves. RAKHEL is shaken, but resolved. After a moment, RAKHEL exits, as well. RACHEL, RASHI and SHLOMO appear from upstage; THEY have been listening surreptitiously. THEY move downstage.)

RACHEL: So this is your idea of fun?

RASHI: You need to look at all sides of a story, Rachel.

RACHEL: I can't believe he would threaten her like that!

RASHI: Young men and women didn't have as much freedom to choose their partners back then. Those who broke with societal customs faced severe consequences.

RACHEL: But she's doing what she thinks is right!

RASHI: And what about you? Does being "right" ever get you into trouble?

> (Pause. RACHEL is stumped.)

SHLOMO: (writing) Her face says "yes".

RACHEL: Enough about me!
    (Pointing)

Is this the way to Akiba's place?

> (SHE starts to move in that direction.)

RASHI: Why?

RACHEL: I have a feeling Rakhel's headed to see Akiba now, and...

> (doing her best imitation of RASHI)

..."if we don't move quickly, we'll miss the fun."

> (SHE exits. Pause.)

SHLOMO: She's got you down!

RASHI: (with confidence)
It's working.
> (HE nods his head in the direction of RACHEL. HE and SHLOMO exit together, quickly. The scene shifts back to the hills outside Jerusalem. RAKHEL is in tears. AKIBA is comforting her.)

AKIBA: Rest your head, darling.

RAKHEL: It's not fair.

AKIBA: I know.

RAKHEL: Why couldn't he just say "yes"? Why, just one time, once in my entire life, could he not accept me for who I am?

AKIBA: You know you cannot live for his blessing. Not if we are to marry.

> (Pause. RAKHEL's eyes well up with more tears. She cries out loud a little more.)

Your pain will only be lessened if you love your father for who he is.

RAKHEL: He is a bully! And all he cares about is money. He would have me marry the sort of man who gives his betrothed a Jerusalem of Gold.

AKIBA: (laughing, in spite of himself)
A Jerusalem of Gold!? You mean those silly tiaras shaped like rooftops of the city?

RAKHEL: Aren't they ridiculous?

AKIBA: I saw a new bride wearing one. Very rich. She looked like—

RAKHEL: (mixed signals)
—a queen!

(Pause.)

AKIBA: You want one.

RAKHEL: I do not.

AKIBA: You do.

RAKHEL: I do not!

AKIBA: (after a moment)
Well, if that's what's required.

(HE picks up some straw.)

RAKHEL: What are you doing?

AKIBA: (weaving the straw together)
Following the fashion, as best I can.

RAKHEL: (uncomprehending)

What?

> [Song: "A CROWN OF STRAW"]

AKIBA: (freely and teasingly)
Every woman of your rank
Or so I'm told
Should expect her love to give her
A Jerusalem of Gold
So I won't complain if you should find it
Reason to withdraw
When you learn the gift I've made for you
Is just a crown of straw

I'd understand if you don't want it.

> (At last, a smile breaks across her face.
> SHE tenderly takes his "gift".)

RACHEL:
A crown of straw,
A crown of straw
More precious than the finest crown of gold
You ever saw
More perfect than a diamond
That shines without a flaw
Darling, I swear, I would rather wear
A crown of straw

> (SHE puts it on. The music continues softly. RAKHEL and AKIBA begin a playful "wedding" dance. RACHEL, RASHI and SHLOMO appear downstage.)

RASHI: So?

A Talmud Tale

RACHEL: Yes, now he loves her.

RASHI: It took time.
> (HE nods at SHLOMO.)

RACHEL: I still find it amazing that she would sacrifice herself like that for him. Not that he isn't cute.

RASHI: Rachel, her greatest sacrifice is yet to come.

RACHEL: What do you mean? She's not going to die, is she?

RASHI: (shakes his head "no")
Watch!

> (RAKHEL and AKIBA stop dancing.
> MUSIC continues under.)

RAKHEL: You're a dancer, too!

AKIBA: With sheep, it helps to be nimble on one's feet.

RAKHEL: (cautiously broaching a new subject)
And what if, say, you were no longer a shepherd?

AKIBA: Me? I'm bound to my sheep till the day I die.

RAKHEL: What if you were not, bound?

AKIBA: What are you saying?

RAKHEL: You may wear the clothes of a shepherd, but beneath them, behind the shepherd's crook, there is someone else. Someone like no other. You have the seeds of greatness in you.. But seedlings don't bear fruit unless they're cultivated. A man of the fields must know that... I have a proposal.

AKIBA: One proposal today is not enough?

RAKHEL: We will marry. And afterwards, you will leave these fields, and go study Torah.

AKIBA: Study Torah?!

RAKHEL: At a Beit Midrash. Go and cultivate those seeds.

AKIBA: Go to the study house and leave you here? All alone? Because, you know if we go through with this, your father's going to cut you off. He won't give you the time of day, let alone a penny.

RAKHEL: Strangely, I'm looking forward to that part of it. It's time I stood on my own two feet.

AKIBA: You are serious.

RAKHEL: But you will return to Jerusalem a learned man! A greater scholar than any man! And I will still be here, waiting for you.

AKIBA: If it's a scholar that you want, perhaps you should marry one of those well brought up men—

RAKHEL: —What they know, you can learn. What you have, only God can give.

AKIBA: I see in your eyes that you will not have this any other way.

RAKHEL: You see well. Oh! There's only one thing more you'll need.

> Every student of the Torah
> So they say
> Might expect a fancy *talit*
> To enfold him on his way
> But the only shawl I have to give's
> The one upon my back

And my love must somehow answer for
Whatever it may lack

(SHE offers him her shawl.)

(teasingly) "And I'd understand if you don't want—"

(Smiling, HE stops her with his hand and lovingly takes the shawl. HE drapes it on his shoulders.)

AKIBA:

A simple shawl,
A simple shawl
More gorgeous than the royal robes
Of Solomon and Saul
Though wealthy men wear linen
While wailing at the wall
When called to prayer, I would rather wear
A simple shawl

(The music swells up into a louder, faster version of the song. AKIBA and RAKHEL dance a second time, a passionate dance of "acceptance.")

RAKHEL	AKIBA
A crown of straw,	A simple shawl,
A crown of straw	A simple shawl
More precious than the finest	More gorgeous than the royal
Crown of gold you ever saw	Robes of Solomon and Saul
More perfect than a diamond	Though wealthy men wear linen
That shines without a flaw	At the wall

RAKHEL: Akiba... My husband!

AKIBA: Rakhel... My wife!

    (The music swells to a loud conclusion. RAKHEL and AKIBA walk off upstage, holding hands.)

[End of song.]

    (RACHEL trails the couple to the horizon, and stares until she can see them no more. RASHI and SHLOMO observe RACHEL's fascination with the events.)

RACHEL: So?

RASHI: So?

RACHEL: So he left her?

RASHI: The next day. Traveled—

SHLOMO: —eighty-five miles. On foot.

RACHEL: (suddenly emotional)
I don't believe you. I don't believe any of this!

RASHI: Rachel, it happened. It's right there in the Talmud.

RACHEL: How do you know? I thought you didn't even live until the 11th century!

    (RASHI is flustered. HE turns to SHLOMO.)

SHLOMO: I think our Rachel was expecting a different outcome to the story.

RASHI: (to Rachel)

Would it help you to know that to be married to a scholar, back then, was regarded as the highest honor?

RACHEL: And what did "honor" get Akiba's Rakhel? Tell me! Loneliness? Poverty? What's the "honor" in that?

RASHI: Stick around, you'll find out.

RACHEL: No! I'm leaving.

RASHI: Hold on.

RACHEL: I'm going to help Rakhel!

RASHI: Not possible!

RACHEL: (taking off her robe)
She could probably use this robe.

       (SHLOMO moves to block her exit.)

RASHI: Rachel, stop! Listen! You can't change history. You can only learn from it.

       (Pause.)

RACHEL: Okay, I'm sorry.

       (SHLOMO helps her put her robe back on.)

RASHI: Don't be sorry. Be elated.

SHLOMO: (clarifying for her) Happy.

RASHI: You not only understand the Talmud, you're moved by it. Come, we must follow Akiba.

RACHEL: But what about Rakhel?

RASHI: We'll see her again, and she'll be fine. Trust me.

RACHEL: I trust you, Rashi. But you are a shnook!

> (BLACKOUT. Time travel music. Scene shifts to the Beit Midrash, some time later. It is late at night. RABBI ELIEZER, a regal older man, is in the midst of fending off one of his students, MEIR. RABBI ELIEZER is cranky, but lovable.)

RABBI ELIEZER: Meir, so many questions!

MEIR: Just one more, Rabbi. Do you really think that an oven cannot be purified after the sun goes down?

RABBI ELIEZER: What are you, baking cookies? Tomorrow's another day!

MEIR: Yes, Rabbi.

> (HE leaves, reluctantly.)

RABBI ELIEZER: Ach, these boys never stop.

> (There is a knock at the door. ELIEZER shouts to be heard.)

What now?!

AKIBA: (from outside)
I'm here to see the Rabbi.

RABBI ELIEZER: Who is it? It's late!

AKIBA: (through the door)

My name's Akiba. Please!

RABBI ELIEZER: (mumbling as he crosses to the door)
Akiba? This should mean something to me? Does a Rabbi's day never end?

(HE opens the door.)

AKIBA: Thank you for opening the door.

RABBI ELIEZER: What is it?

AKIBA: Are you... Rabbi Eliezer?

RABBI ELIEZER: Who else should I be?

AKIBA: I'm honored.

RABBI ELIEZER: And I, Stranger, am exhausted. So please tell me why you've come. You don't seem like our usual sort of visitor.

AKIBA: I'm sure I'm not. I've come to study Torah, unlikely as it seems.

RABBI ELIEZER: (to heaven)
God, is this one a hungry mind, or just another hungry mouth?

AKIBA: I'm not looking for a meal, Rabbi. Please, hear me out. I've been walking for days. I've already been turned away from three other study houses!

RABBI ELIEZER: Why did the others turn you away?

AKIBA: At the first, they said I was too old. The second, too dirty. The last one was simply too crowded. And always the same advice: "Go back to your flock!"

RABBI ELIEZER: (To heaven again, distraught) He's a shepherd!

AKIBA: All my forty years.

RABBI ELIEZER: So why come to study, at this late date?

AKIBA: Because I've made a vow. To my bride. To learn Torah. How can I break my vow and be worthy of calling myself her husband?

RABBI ELIEZER: A vow to one's beloved is not something to be taken lightly. You are a wise fellow for knowing that at least.

AKIBA: I would not take any vow lightly. And Rakhel, my wife, is sacrificing much to make my study possible.

RABBI ELIEZER: Your Rakhel must be a righteous woman.

AKIBA: That she is. And I will not let her down.

RABBI ELIEZER: You know the study of Torah is a life long commitment. A road that only begins here at the Beit Midrash.

AKIBA: I'm a shepherd. Patience comes with the territory.

RABBI ELIEZER: You're an unusual man, Akiba.

(HE considers him a moment.)

I presume you can read and write?

(AKIBA doesn't answer.)

Or, at least....read?

AKIBA: I can read the tracks of a sheep who has strayed from my flock. Or the movement of the stars in the night sky. I've slept out enough nights to be expert at that.

RABBI ELIEZER: I begin to see why the others suggested you go back to your sheep. To begin from scratch at this late date...

AKIBA: I've never been afraid of hard work!

RABBI ELIEZER: I believe you Akiba. Still, there is yet another problem. Here at the Beit Midrash, everyone must have a study partner. And, considering you can't even read, with whom, in good conscience, could I pair you up?

[Song: " BOTH SIDES OF AN ISSUE"]

RABBI ELIEZER:

> In the first place, you don't know anything
> So what kind of partner would you be?
> On the other hand, that could make you curious
> Dying to look and see
>
> So on the one hand, you might be a burden
> A truly unnecessary job
> On the other hand, this could be a bit of a mitzvah
> Even a gift from God
>
> Seeing both sides of an issue
> Is what studying's about
> You can never know the answer
> Till you've turned it inside out
> Look at both sides of an issue
> And before the day is through
> You'll see sides, and sides of sides,
> You never knew
>
> (HE dances a little dance as HE sings a niggun)
>
> Lai- lai- lai- lai lai lai
> Lai- lai- lai- lai lai
> Lai- lai- lai- lai lai lai
>
> (RABBI ELIEZER looks for an example to use.)

Take this bottle of wine, Akiba. Would you say it was half empty or half full?

AKIBA: Well....on the one hand....if one had a lot of guests to serve, and only this one bottle, then I would call it half empty. On the other hand, if just you and I were to have the pleasure of polishing it off alone, then it is definitely half full—since it leaves us plenty to share!

RABBI ELIEZER: A not unimpressive bit of reasoning, Akiba! Perhaps you are already starting to—.
    (catches himself).
—still...

  On the one hand, you're over forty
  And you don't even know your alef-beit

AKIBA:

  On the other hand, I have real experience
  Could be, that carries weight

BOTH

  So on the one hand

RABBI ELIEZER:

  You are like a blank slate

AKIBA:

  No writing recorded there to read

RABBI ELIEZER:

  On the other hand
  You are like a sample of truth

AKIBA:

  With ev'ry life example you need

  Seeing both sides of an issue

> Is what studying's about
> Well, the concept is no stranger than,
> Say, breathing in and out
> Start on one side of an issue
> But before you make it through
> You'll find someone else's side
> Belongs to you!
>
> Lai- lai- lai- lai lai lai
> Lai- lai- lai- lai lai
> Lai- lai- lai- lai lai lai!

I know how a shepherd learns his trade, Rabbi. But tell me, how does a Jew grow wise?

RABBI ELIEZER: A wise Jew is one who learns from absolutely everyone!

> So, say I take a chance
> Attempt a diff'rent way
> Presume that since you've lived a lot
> You've got a lot to say
>
> Yes, if I take a leap
> Into the great unknown

AKIBA:
> Since you've got me with you
> You're not doing it alone!

Rabbi, tell me please, what makes a Jew strong?

RABBI ELIEZER: A strong Jew is one who subdues his evil impulses.

AKIBA: And when is a Jew considered rich?
RABBI ELIEZER: A rich Jew is one who is content with his lot. Now, let me ask YOU one...What Jew will be honored?

AKIBA: (after a moment's thought) The one who honors others!

RABBI ELIEZER: And say I tried you out as a partner.... for myself!

(MUSIC out.)

AKIBA: Then there'd be no man more honored than I!

(MUSIC.)

BOTH:
Seeing both sides of an issue
Is what studying's about
You can never know the answer
Till you've turned it inside out

Start on one side of an issue
And before you've reached the end
You might find that you have found
Yourself a friend!

Lai- lai- lai- lai lai lai
Lai- lai- lai- lai lai
Lai- lai- lai- lai lai lai!

AKIBA: May I stay then, Rabbi?

RABBI ELIEZER: Akiba, it is I who would be honored!
(THEY shake on it.)

[end of song]

(AKIBA and RABBI ELIEZER recede into silhouette as RASHI and SHLOMO take focus. THEY are engaged in a heated argument.)

SHLOMO: Why, you overbearing, sanctimonious, second-rate Philistine!

RASHI: Oh, well that makes you a sniveling, disobedient, pencil-snatching little bookworm!

> (RASHI and SHLOMO look over their shoulders to see if they have caught RACHEL's attention. RASHI signals SHLOMO to continue.)

SHLOMO: Furthermore, next time you want to engage in fact-fiddling, better bring your own eraser!

> (RACHEL tears herself away from observing AKIBA and ELIEZER and moves to RASHI and SHLOMO.)

RACHEL: What is going on?

SHLOMO: He tried to manipulate the record!

RASHI: (to her)
I am protecting you.
            (to SHLOMO, referring to RACHEL)
She is not ready!

SHLOMO: She is ripe and ready!

> (Rapid-fire, as previously:)

RASHI:		RACHEL:
Not ready.	(simultaneously)	Excuse me.

SHLOMO:	RACHEL:
Ripe and ready!	Excuse me!

RASHI:
Not.

RACHEL:
May I say something?

SHLOMO: Ready or not, she is—

RASHI: —neither ripe, nor ready.   RACHEL: Would you please stop!

SHLOMO: She is ready, ripe and rarin' to go!

RACHEL: I said, stop!

(On the word "stop" RACHEL busts apart RASHI and SHLOMO who have nearly come to "blows".)

RACHEL: (to RASHI)
Maybe you could explain what it is that I am not ready for?

RASHI: Every student of the Talmud reaches a point when he or she might engage in debate. Rachel, I feel you have a ways to go.

RACHEL: I can debate.

RASHI: Debate requires not only a mastery of the facts but an ability to make arguments based on logic. There's little room for hot-blooded emotion.

SHLOMO: (to HER) Or so he says.

RACHEL: Try me.

RASHI: Huh?

RACHEL: Try me! You say I'm not ready, I say, try me!

RASHI: (false reluctance)
Well okay, we will.
     (HE winks at SHLOMO.

> MUSIC under: "AM I RIGHT?")

What portion of the scriptures were you reading?

RACHEL: Jacob and the ladder.

RASHI: Good. Sit. We'll ask some questions.

SHLOMO: You'll give some answers.

RASHI: Ready?

RACHEL: Hit me with your best bat mitzvah quiz! Just, please, no questions about sushi or prime rib.

(LIGHTS shift to another part of the stage where RACHEL'S MOTHER is talking on a cell phone.)

MOTHER: You're telling me it's maddening! I mean, my own daughter acting all high and mighty! (Listens) I have told her that! Making it elegant doesn't negate the spiritual significance (Listens.) No, like a brick wall. (Listens, and agrees) Well put! "A family event." And it reflects on all of us!

> (MOTHER sings.)

[Song: "AM I RIGHT?"]

So, she should listen just a little bit at least, am I right?

> (Lights come back up on RACHEL,
> RASHI and SHLOMO, while remaining
> on MOTHER.)

RASHI: Who was Jacob's father?

RACHEL: Isaac! That's easy.

(MOTHER, in her world, continues to sing into phone.)

MOTHER:
It's not like I'm campaigning for a priest, am I right?

SHLOMO: Esau and Rebecca?

RACHEL: Brother and mother!

MOTHER:
I'll end the day demented or deceased, am I right?
I am asking, am I wrong or am I right?

(Lights dim on HER.)

RASHI: And how did Jacob get his father's blessing?

RACHEL: (thinking)
His father's blessing...his father's blessing...hmmm

(LIGHTS shift to another part of the stage where a troubled BEN KALBA SAVUA stands beside his lieutenant, BEN DAVID, pronounced, "DaVEED".)

BEN KALBA SAVUA: Ben David, you're a sensible young man...

BEN DAVID: I try to be.

BEN KALBA SAVUA (not really asking): You don't think I've overreacted, do you?

BEN DAVID (unsure how to respond): Well...

BEN KALBA SAVUA: (Sings)

> Rakhel is fasting when she should have had a feast,
> Am I right?
> My beauty is cavorting with a beast, am I right?
> He's a shepherd but it's I who has been fleeced, am I right?
> I am asking, am I wrong or am I right?
>
> (LIGHTS add on RACHEL's MOTHER again. Both parents sing, each in their own world.)

BOTH PARENTS:
> Why do children always think that they know better
> They're a blessing that's more like a blight
> Breaking ev'ry last law to the letter

MOTHER: (into cell phone)
> Am I wrong?

BEN KALBA SAVUA:
> Am I right?
>
> (Lights dim on THEM. Back up on RACHEL, RASHI, SHLOMO.)

RASHI: Where did Jacob flee to avoid Esau's revenge?

RACHEL: (getting more excited) Charan!

SHLOMO: What did he use as a pillow when he stopped to rest?

RACHEL: A stone!

RASHI: And what did he dream about?
RACHEL: (triumphant) A ladder full of angels!!

(LIGHTS shift, back up on BEN KALBA
SAVUA and RACHEL's MOTHER.
THEY sing, each in their own world.)

BEN KALBA SAVUA:
She's unmoving, though I've prodded, pushed and pleaded

MOTHER: (into phone)
She's contrary but never contrite!

BOTH:
Leaving "honor thy father/mother" unheeded

MOTHER:
Am I wrong?

BOTH:
Am I right?

(Lights back up on RACHEL, RASHI, SHLOMO.)

RACHEL:
I guess this means I'm ready to debate, am I right?

RASHI:
I can't see any reason she should wait, am I right?

SHLOMO (to RASHI)
She may even put some Midrash in the Beit, am I right?

RACHEL, RASHI, SHLOMO, MOTHER, KALBA SAVUA
(still in their separate worlds)
I am asking,
Am I wrong or am I right?

MOTHER, KALBA SAVUA
(separate worlds)

>Only asking,
>Am I wrong or am I.....

RASHI: Congratulations, Rachel. You are ready!

RACHEL: I told ya so!

MOTHER, KALBA SAVUA
>(separate worlds)
>....Right.....?

>(MOTHER mimes saying goodbye to the friend, shuts her cell phone, exits; KALBA SAVUA pats BEN DAVID on the shoulder and escorts him off; RASHI, SHLOMO and RACHEL move a bit closer to the entrance to the study house.)

[End of song.]

RASHI: Now, when we enter the study house—

RACHEL: —enter?

RASHI: You said you're ready for a debate. When we enter the study house to begin the debate, you'll find Akiba seated next to Rabbi Eliezer. You'll take your place next to—

RACHEL: —my place?

RASHI: You'll take your temporary spiritual place next to Rabbi Eliezer.

RACHEL: (nervously) Okay.

>(AKIBA and RABBI ELIEZER reappear at the Beit Midrash. In mime, they are engaged in heated debate. The theme of

"BOTH SIDES OF AN ISSUE" plays.)

RASHI: It's several months later. Akiba has learned to read and write, and he and Rabbi Eliezer are discussing the Jacob story. Relax, Rachel. And remember, the Talmud is a place where all your questions are welcome. Ready?

RACHEL: (taking a deep breath)
Ready.

> (RACHEL enters the study house and scurries over to a seat next to RABBI ELIEZER and AKIBA. THEY don't seem aware of her yet. MUSIC out.)

AKIBA: (exasperated) No, no, no, no. You still don't see my point!

RABBI ELIEZER: I'm listening!

AKIBA: It's simple. Jacob wakes up. He's confused. He's frightened. He's shaken by the power of his own dream! So he says, "God really must have been right here in this place, and I, I did not know."

RABBI ELIEZER: But why the two "I"s, Akiba? "And I" ? that's number one—, "I", —that's number two—"did not know."

AKIBA: I... don't know.

RABBI ELIEZER: (HE chuckles.) You don't know? Try this: maybe Jacob thinks too much about Jacob! So he is saying, "God was here all along, and the reason I didn't notice, is I was too busy paying attention to myself!"

AKIBA: (impressed) Very good, Rabbi!

RABBI ELIEZER: (HE laughs harder.) Your reading and writing have improved, my friend, but there is so much more yet to learn!

A Talmud Tale

[Song: "WHAT DOES IT MEAN?"]

(HE dances a bit as he sings):

LAI-LAI-LAI-LAI-LAI
LAI-LAI-LAI-LAI-LA

(RACHEL, wanting to keep track of their discussion, looks around for some "scratch paper" to take notes on. Finally, SHE grabs some of the pink invitations for her bat mitzvah to use.)

AKIBA: I confess, the Holy Book still feels to me like... an unsolvable mystery!

RABBI ELIEZER: No, no! A wonderful mystery! (AKIBA shakes his head, at a loss.) And there is a way in— with one simple question: (HE sings)

What does it mean?"

AKIBA: "What does it mean?"

RABBI ELIEZER:
    What the text says, it says in words
    But what do they mean?

AKIBA:
    What do they mean?

RABBI ELIEZER:
    Is there a reason that a stone serves for a pillow?
    Is Jacob dreaming or are all these visions real?

AKIBA:
    What is the meaning of a ladder full of angels?

RABBI ELIEZER:
> How did hearing God address him

BOTH
> Make JACOB feel?

RABBI ELIEZER:
> What does all of this mean, do you suppose?
> The closer you look, the more your interest grows
> Read the lines, but also in-between
> To find an answer to: "What does it mean?"

> (MUSIC continues under.)

AKIBA: You're right, Rabbi. I need to look deeper.

RABBI ELIEZER: Don't be so hard on yourself. It takes years to unlock the meaning of Torah. Look at me, sixty years old, and still unlocking!

AKIBA: At least you have a key.

RABBI ELIEZER: When it comes to opening the gates of Heaven, there is no shortage of keys. Not now, not before, and not in the future!

> (With these words, RACHEL feels moved, puts her notes away, and is poised to contribute to the discussion. Similarly, RASHI, feeling compelled to be involved, moves closer to the others.)

RACHEL: Speaking of the future, may I?

> (RABBI ELIEZER and AKIBA turn and see her)

AKIBA: There are girls here at the Beit Midrash!

RABBI ELIEZER: So it would seem!! Who are you, Child?

RACHEL: I'm Rachel...uh...."Rakhel."

RABBI ELIEZER: (To AKIBA) Your Rakhel?!

RACHEL and AKIBA: No!

RACHEL: Rakhel Cohen.

RABBI ELIEZER: Oh, a "bat Kohein!" ("Daughter of the priestly class.") Where are you from?

RACHEL: Lower Manhattan*. (*Her answer can match the actual location where the musical is being performed.)

RABBI ELIEZER and AKIBA: Where?!

RASHI: (stepping into the fray) Maybe you should ask her "When she's from!"

RABBI ELIEZER: You again!

RASHI: Miss Cohen is a new friend of mine.

RABBI ELIEZER: And this is Akiba, a new friend of mine, since you last came.

RASHI: A pleasure to meet you, Akiba. The name's Rashi.

RABBI ELIEZER: One of our very active colleagues from...which century will it be again?

RASHI: From the year, 4850.
               (turns to RACHEL)
Eleventh Century, C.E., as you call it.
               (To the OTHERS)
And Rachel here comes some nine hundred years later.

AKIBA: What's happening, Rabbi?!

RABBI ELIEZER: Don't look so stupefied, my friend. Torah study is quite unbound by time or space.

RACHEL: So then...may I sit at the table with you?

> (RABBI ELIEZER hesitates...SHE is a girl.)

RASHI: (THEY have had this conversation! Warningly) Rabbi Eliezer?!

AKIBA: (chiming in) Here, why don't you look on with me?

> (HE shares his book with RACHEL.)

RASHI: (verbally nudging RABBI ELIEZER to continue) Well, Rabbi?

> (THEY sing again.)

RABBI ELIEZER: (to RACHEL)
What does it mean?

RACHEL: (considering)
What does it mean?

RABBI ELIEZER:
All these stories, so full of life
But what do they mean?

RACHEL:
What do they mean?

AKIBA: Could we go back to the beginning, Rabbi? I know I must have overlooked something in Isaac's upbringing.

RABBI ELIEZER: Always blaming it on the parents!

A Talmud Tale

>(MUSIC continues under; RABBI
>ELIEZER and AKIBA continue their
>"argument"/ discussion in mime.)

RACHEL: Psst! Rashi! I just realized. I'm not as lost as I think I am!

RASHI: Good, Rachel!

RACHEL: I mean, Akiba's just trying to figure it out like me.

RASHI: Exactly! And every soul that's born has something special to add!

RACHEL: (with confidence, now)
Well, do you know why I think Jacob used the word "I" twice?

RASHI: No, why? Tell me! Tell them!
>(To the OTHERS)

Gentleman, listen: another take on your oft-quoted line!

>(RABBI ELIEZER and AKIBA cease
>their arguing, having reached no mutual
>conclusion. THEY stop to hear RACHEL)

RACHEL: Okay, here's what I think: The first "I" stands for "individual", that is, "I", or Jacob alone, "did not know." The second "I" stands for "infinite".

RABBI ELIEZER: "Infinite?"

RACHEL: Yes, infinite—
>(MUSIC out. RACHEL proceeds, very
>rapidly and excitedly:)

—as in the infinite number of people who think they know everything when in fact they know not much more than I do, which is to say very little other than what we think we know or in other words, Jacob is expressing the frustration and happiness that we all would naturally feel if we woke up to suddenly face the eternal presence of an all-knowing, all-powerful, and almighty God!

> (RACHEL emits a self-satisfied grin. RASHI, AKIBA, and RABBI ELIEZER are dumbstruck.)

RASHI: Well, that's a new one.
> (Pause.)

RABBI ELIEZER: I love it!

> (During the final chorus, RABBI ELIEZER remains mesmerized by RACHEL'S interpretation.)

RASHI, AKIBA, RACHEL:
What does all of this mean, do you suppose?

RACHEL:
The closer I look, the more my interest grows

RASHI, AKIBA, RACHEL:
Read the lines, but also in-between

RACHEL:
To find an answer to:

RASHI, AKIBA
More than one answer to:

RACHEL:
A different answer to:

ALL:
"What does it mean?"

> (MUSIC continues under.)

RASHI: Well, it's been a pleasure as always. Rachel, come.

RACHEL: (to RABBI ELIEZER and AKIBA) Thank you!

RASHI: (to RABBI ELIEZER and AKIBA) Shalom Aleichem.

RABBI ELIEZER: Aleichem Shalom.

> (RASHI and RACHEL exit the Beit Midrash and offstage. SHLOMO follows. AKIBA stands as if to exit too.)

AKIBA: I'm turning in, Rabbi…Uh, do you know what our weather will be like tomorrow?

RABBI ELIEZER: Not a clue, Akiba. Not a clue.

[End of song.]

> (BLACKOUT. RACHEL reappears alone in a spot of light. SHE sings.)

[Song: "SO MANY QUESTIONS (Reprise)"]

RACHEL:
> So many questions
> How can we ever agree?
> Still, what a surprise
> That these ancient guys
> Think that they might learn from me!
>
> So many questions
> Are suddenly sort of fun
> Maybe I can answer just one…

[End of song.]

>   (Her MOTHER enters excitedly with a shopping bag from Bloomingdales.)

MOTHER: Rachel! I have it! I have the answer! Right here in this bag. I am so relieved!

RACHEL: Me too, Mom. It's finally starting to make sense! About Jacob and the ladder. Rashi says that every soul is born with something special to add to what's already been said—

>   (MOTHER reaches into the bag and pulls out a pair of bright pink silk pants.)

MOTHER: —Tada! Are these heaven, or what?

RACHEL: (stopped in her tracks) What are they?

MOTHER: What do you mean, what are they? They're pants! And they're pink! Talk about the perfect solution.

RACHEL: Mom, you didn't—

MOTHER: —I know you don't like me to shop for you, but just as I was leaving the store, there they were, staring at me on the clearance rack and, well, I couldn't pass them up. I mean, just look! They're perfect!

RACHEL: For what?

MOTHER: Rachel, I am doing my best to meet you half way. Hand me those invitations.

>   (RACHEL hands her the pile of pink invitations.)

See? It's the exact same pink! I mean, I almost flipped—

>   (SHE stops dead.)

A Talmud Tale

Oh, my God. Oh, my God! Tell me you didn't use these for scratch paper!

RACHEL: (hadn't really realized) Oh, well…just a few of them, I guess. I mean, Rabbi Eliezer was interpreting my Torah portion and you know, he's one of the greatest rabbis of all time—

MOTHER: —You think this is all a big joke. Do you have any idea how much one of these costs?

RACHEL: No.
MOTHER: These aren't "Post-it®s!"
        (SHE demonstrates by putting one against
        her forehead, it doesn't stick, of course.)

RACHEL: I'm sorry.

MOTHER: I cannot believe that you would take engraved invitations and just scribble on them.

RACHEL: I wasn't scribbling. I was taking notes.

MOTHER: I have tried… and tried and tried to compromise. But no matter how hard I try, you just want to make a mockery of me!

RACHEL: (really hurt) I said I was sorry…. But, you know, I'm not the one making a mockery! I thought my bat mitzvah was supposed to mean something. But you keep trying to turn it into— I don't know what—a fashion show or something.

MOTHER: (stung) That is truly demeaning! Did it ever occur to you that maybe I take this all so seriously because I care so much! This is not just your day, you know. This is very much a family affair.

RACHEL: Maybe you should just have your own bat mitzvah.

MOTHER: When I was your age, young lady, I was not given that option!

(SHE storms out. RACHEL looks down at the Talmud book she has been holding and lets out a gasp of frustration.)

RACHEL: Aargh!..Rashi, where are you?

(RASHI and SHLOMO have entered.)

RASHI: Over here.

RACHEL: Here. I don't need this.

(SHE hands him the book.)

RASHI: You don't need the Talmud?

RABBI: No. And I don't think I can go through with it. The bat mitzvah.

RASHI: You're not one for adversity, are you?

RACHEL: Adversity?

RASHI: Discomfort.

SHLOMO: Misfortune.

RASHI: Hardship!

RACHEL: Why are you blaming me? Didn't you hear what my mother just said? She hates me!

(SHE is in tears. Pause. RASHI looks at SHLOMO. Pause. RASHI gestures to SHLOMO as if to say "help her." SHLOMO walks over to RACHEL and slowly extends his arms towards her as if inviting her to hug him. RACHEL

(collapses into SHLOMO's arms in a manner that surprises him.)

SHLOMO: There, there.

RASHI: Rachel, your mother doesn't hate you. But I do believe she's frustrated.

RACHEL: And I'm not?!

(SHLOMO gently tries to extricate himself from RACHEL's grip but she is clinging hard to him.)

RASHI: (seeing an opening) Well, can you imagine how frustrated Rakhel must feel right now?

(RACHEL throws SHLOMO off suddenly and is back to her "old self".)

RACHEL: Rakhel at least has Akiba's love, even if they're apart!

RASHI: I agree. But look what else is happening to Rakhel:

(HE points to another part of the stage where RAKHEL is speaking with a PEASANT WOMAN.)

PEASANT WOMAN: If only your father didn't employ my husband, you know I'd let you stay.
RAKHEL: It's all right, I understand. Thank you, anyway.

RASHI: (points to another part of the stage) And listen there.

(BEN KALBA SAVUA appears beside BEN DAVID, his "lieutenant.")

BEN DAVID: Did you know your daughter is sleeping in Nahum Ish Gamzu's shack?

KALBA SAVUA: She is learning the price of defiance!

> [Song: "WELCOME TO THE TALMUD" (Reprise)]

>> (During the musical intro, AKIBA and ENSEMBLE enter and direct themselves presentationally to RACHEL.)

RASHI: (sighing) So you see, Rachel: parents and children — it's as old as time!

SOLO FEMALE ANCIENT
(placing a comforting hand on RAKHEL's shoulder)
> A father oh so stern

SOLO MALE ANCIENT
(referring to AKIBA, who is poring over an open Torah scroll)
> A man with much to learn

ENSEMBLE
> Their stories make you yearn
> To find out what's in store

ALL MALE ANCIENTS
> Through sacrifice and strain

ALL FEMALE ANCIENTS
> Rakhel may someday gain

ENSEMBLE
> But time won't ease the pain
> She feels and can't ignore

A Talmud Tale

> (softly, as the ENSEMBLE slowly moves to surround RACHEL.)

Ooh, ah
Ooh, ah

> (and continuing under:)

RACHEL: All of this happened two thousand years ago! Why should I care about any of it?

RASHI: You do care. And they care about you. Look how you impressed Rabbi Eliezer and Akiba!

> (RABBI ELIEZER and AKIBA smile at RACHEL.)

RACHEL: (sarcastic) I'm great with ancient people.

RASHI: And they might just help you find the answer to your dilemma.

RACHEL: I don't need your help!

ENSEMBLE
> Welcome to the Talmud
> Welcome to our choir
> We come to enlighten
> Inform and inspire!

RACHEL: (hands over ears) Please go! All of you!
RASHI: Give up now, and who knows if you'll ever find out what happened to Rakhel and Akiba.

ENSEMBLE
> Oh welcome, and please
> Consider it—

RACHEL: **Goodbye!**

> (With a wave of RACHEL's hand, the MUSIC comes to an abrupt halt.)

I'm sorry.

> (The MUSIC resumes softly. All ANCIENTS slowly disappear except RASHI, who faces RACHEL silently for a moment. He places RACHEL's Talmud book down beside her, then turns and leaves. RACHEL watches him go, then looks back towards the book. SHE closes it. LIGHTS FADE TO BLACK.)

[END OF ACT ONE]

ACT TWO

> (LIGHTS UP on RACHEL seated in RABBI's office, writing feverishly on her note pad. RABBI, seated across his desk from RACHEL, is reading something and appears distracted. A few beats of mad scribbling pass before RACHEL speaks:)

RACHEL: I can't believe how easy this is!

RABBI: Good. Keep going.

> (RACHEL loudly flips a "finished" page over and begins writing at the top of a new page.)

RACHEL: This pad is definitely not blank!

RABBI: I'm very glad the ideas are so free-flowing for you, Rachel.

RACHEL: Its like, I'm not blocked!

RABBI: And whenever you're ready to share it, I'd love to—

RACHEL: —one more thing.
> (Finishing a sentence emphatically, SHE stops writing and looks up, self-satisfied.)

There!

RABBI: Okay! Now read it to me. Just the way you'd want it heard.

RACHEL: May I stand?

RABBI: Of course!

> (Summoning courage, RACHEL stands,

> faces forward, finds the first page,
> and begins reading slowly and loudly:)

RACHEL: "Dear Mom,

> [Song: "THE PERFECT MOTHER"
> MUSIC under.]

I know that lately we've been fighting a lot. I think the pressure of the bat mitzvah was getting to both of us, for different reasons. But if we both want to go through with it, and I believe we do, I think we can reach an understanding, and that would please our whole family.

RABBI: Excellent!

RACHEL: So look, I promise to stop locking myself in my room every night. All I ask is that you read this short list—(SHE flips the page over excitedly)—this short list of changes I'd like you to make."

> (During the song, her brother, STUART
> and her friend, SARAH, appear to sing
> backup [see score], as if in her imagination.
> THEY disappear when the song ends.)

RABBI: Uh, Rachel—

RACHEL: —Wait, this is the good part!

> (SHE sings:)

Don't say you know
What I should wear
Don't even try to suggest
What you think is best for my hair

Don't say I'll need
A padded bra

> Or tons of creams
> Just to cover up the tiniest flaw.
>
> Don't say I can't
> Have certain friends
> When all I've got are my friends
> And I wouldn't want any other
> But if you'd change
> These few small things
> Then, you'd be
> On your way to becoming
> The perfect mother

RABBI: Well, Rachel, that's, that's—

RACHEL: —Do you think it's too strong?

RABBI: Well, I told you to be honest.

> (As the scene continues, MOTHER, dressed in a terry-cloth bathrobe, enters the kitchen of the Cohen house, where an envelope awaits her on the table. It's before her bedtime, and the envelope surprises her. SHE opens it and begins to silently read the letter that RACHEL is in the process of writing. SHE is caught off guard and is alarmed by the tone of the letter. SHE makes various faces as she reads through the equivalent of the first section of the song from above.)

RACHEL: It's very honest!

RABBI: Maybe you could tone it down a bit? Keep it positive?

RACHEL: Good idea.

RABBI: Talk about what's important to you. Why you want to do the ceremony your way. What the party should be like, and why.

RACHEL: Yes, yes! Say no more!

(SHE begins to write again.)

MOTHER: (reading aloud) "And as far as my party goes,"

RACHEL	MOTHER:
(singing as she continues to "write")	(wearily)
Don't stop the band	Don't stop the band
At four o'clock	At four o'clock
When four o'clock's the hour	
That the band	
Really starts to rock	When we're picking up the trash?
Don't say we can't	Don't say you can't
Make too much noise	Make too much noise
If all that means is	
You haven't conquered	
Your fear of boys	So now you're a shrink?
There's one boy Bob	Oh please, not Bob!
—You know which one—	He set a fire in our house!
Well that boy Bob's gotta come	
'Cause I consider him like a brother	Over my dead body!
If you'd agree	If I'd agree
To everything	Not to Bob!
Then you'd be	I would be
On your way	On my way
To becoming	To becoming
The perfect mother	The perfect mother

A Talmud Tale

> (During this next passage, MOTHER searches the kitchen for her own paper and pen, finds both, and will begin drafting her own answer to RACHEL's letter.)

RABBI: Rachel, I don't know that you're taking the right approach.

RACHEL: Should I just tell it to her face-to-face?

RABBI: No! What I mean is—

RACHEL: —keep it positive?

RABBI: Yes, and before you give it to her, you really ought to soften it. Things go down easier with honey. I have to go.

RACHEL: All right, I'll change it. I promise!

RABBI: Let me know what happens. (HE leaves.)

RACHEL: Let's see.
> (RACHEL rereads what she has written, flips over to a new, blank page, and clicks her pen as she thinks for a moment. In the meantime, MOTHER has pen in hand and is ready.)

MOTHER (**writing**)	RACHEL (**writing**)
Dear Rachel,	Mother: I know
I received your note,	nobody's really perfect
and,	'Cause perfect
to tell the truth,	Is really hard to be.
It's hard for me to understand	Still, I know
How you can think	We can all do better
That you're better off	That's why this letter
without me!	Might
	Help you see another way

(Pausing to consider what to put next)	Or two, or three, if that's okay
	Oh Mom, what I'm trying to say is,
	I could be perfectly happy
I would be perfectly happy to back off	Just being me
Except that I'm your mother, dear	
So trust me, please.	
Especially here.	
I see what's best for you	
As clear as a bell!	
RACHEL	MOTHER:
So scratch the cake	Take a deep breath!
With gobs of frosting	I'm your friend!
Don't spell my name in pink	
And by the way,	
What's all of this costing?	One day, you'll see
I hate balloons	That Mommy knows,
I wanna pop 'em	Mommy cares,
And if they try to hang a piñata,	
I swear I'll stop 'em!	And I always will!
I could go on	I could go on
I'll keep it short	I'll keep this short.
I'll look to	You can
Count on your support	Count on my support
And our love for one another	And my love.
	By the way, you misspelled "pinata".
If you'd just let	If you'd just let me
My life take wing	Take care of everything
Then, you'd be	You would be

On your way,	On your way,
Bet you are	Hope you are
On your way	On your way
To becoming	To becoming
The perfect	The perfect
Mother!	Daughter!
The perfect mother!	Daughter!
The perfect	The perfect
Mother!	Daughter!

[End of song.]

>(Over the final notes, RACHEL and MOTHER fold their letters, place them inside respective envelopes, seal each envelope, write each other's names on the respective envelopes, and throw Nthem down with finality on their respective tables. SONG ends. MOTHER disappears.)

RACHEL: (calling out and looking around) Rashi! Shlomo! Hello?! I think you'd want to know what's going on here! The letter? The one the Rabbi had me write?

>(In one swift motion, SHE makes a "gun" with her hand, points it at her head, and makes a single exploding sound.)

Backfired! I've never seen my mom so steamed! I mean, I thought I could get her to see my point-of-view, but instead, its like she's pretending I don't exist. Come on, guys! Give a girl a break! (trying to lure them out) Say, how are Akiba and Rakhel doing? (A realization.) The book! (SHE looks around frantically for her Talmud book.) Where did I put it? (SHE spots the book.) There! (SHE opens the book. A magical musical chord strikes.) The book is open!

RASHI: (appearing suddenly, arms folded)
Yes, but is the case closed?

> (RACHEL turns to see RASHI and
> SHLOMO, as before. SHLOMO is
> working intensely on a crossword puzzle
> and appears to be engrossed.)

RACHEL: Hey! Boy, am I glad to see— (Pause.) Okay, okay. You were right, I was wrong.

RASHI: And?

RACHEL: And, what you were saying... when I last saw you... something about my "dilemma"?

RASHI: Oh, that you "just might find the answer to your dilemma" in looking at the Talmud.

RACHEL: Yes! That! How does that work?

SHLOMO: (as if "stumped")
Rash, four letters, starting with a "p", map?

RASHI: Plan.

> (SHLOMO enters the word "plan" into his
> crossword puzzle.)

Rachel, nothing is guaranteed.

RACHEL: I'll guarantee you this, in thirty days, I'm either a Bat or an embarrassment!

SHLOMO: Three letters, ends with an "e", bzzzz?

> (Without being too obvious that he knows
> the answer, SHLOMO twirls his

A Talmud Tale

        hand around as if his fingertips were a bee.)

RASHI: **Bee!**

        (SHLOMO gleefully enters "bee" into his puzzle.)

Do you remember when I said to you, "we'll get to your mother later"?

RACHEL: **Yes?**

RASHI: The time has come.

RACHEL: **Huh?**

        (MOTHER, well-dressed, enters down left and faces audience. She is silently talking on a cell phone to a close friend.)

RASHI: To deal with your mother!

RACHEL: **Now?**

RASHI: Now, or never!

        (HE points to MOTHER. RACHEL sees her and is startled.)

MOTHER: (into phone) ...oh I am so glad I called you... Right! I'll tell her that I simply will not be discounted. She has got to acknowledge that this is a group effort. A bat mitzvah is a family affair...Exactly. What can she do? Listen, thanks, sweetie, I'll keep you posted... Okay, bye!

        (SHE pushes "end" on her cell phone. SHE dials a new number and begins a new conversation.)

RACHEL: **Mom!**

RASHI and SHLOMO: She can't hear you.

RACHEL: (a flustered moment, then): Why is she doing this to me?

RASHI: She believes she's doing what's right.

RACHEL: It's not!

RASHI: Ben Kalba Savua thought what he did to Rakhel was right. Rakhel disagreed. Does that make him wrong?

RACHEL: Well, yes! But what does that have to do with—

RASHI: —Shh! You need to hear this:

MOTHER: (into phone) You're telling me it'll be a big cake? I've got 500 people to feed!..And I have the lettering for the top layer, of course! Do you have a pencil?
        (SHE clears her throat.)
"To our Rachel: Roses are red, violets are blue, no one's as wonderfully perfect as you."

RACHEL: (Pause. SHE is horrified. SHE cups her hands over her ears, closes her eyes and screams:) Ahhhh!

    (As MOTHER continues to talk silently with bakery shop employee, SHLOMO silently mouths the words "Plan B" to RASHI while emitting an "aren't-I-clever" grin; RASHI mimics SHLOMO's "bzzz" motion back as if to say, "Do you think I'm stupid?" RACHEL opens her eyes.)

RASHI: Rachel, your situation calls for extreme measures. We've got to act fast.

RACHEL: Okay.

RASHI: Your mother's first name?

RACHEL: Elaine.

SHLOMO: (jotting it in his book) Elaine!

RACHEL: Wait, why?

RASHI: If you don't communicate to your mother what you're feeling about the Talmud, how do you expect her to share in your enthusiasm?

RACHEL: She won't listen!

RASHI: Then she'll just have to come along.

RACHEL: With us? No way!

RASHI: (sharply)
There is no other way!

[Song: "AN OPEN BOOK (Reprise)"]

Open her eyes to what's inside here
She'll be surprised by all she sees
Nothing's gained if nothing is tried here
So be wise, dear:
Say please

(MUSIC continues under.)

RACHEL: "Please, Mom, read this book?"

RASHI: (gesturing to MOTHER, who is wrapping up her conversation)
You'll find the right words.

(HE steps aside.)

MOTHER: It's a pleasure doing business with you, too. Goodbye.

> (SHE pushes "end" on her cell phone, folds it up and turns to exit. RACHEL moves towards her. MUSIC out.)

RACHEL: Mom?

MOTHER: (startled) I thought you were upstairs.

RACHEL: I heard you talking. Look, I'm sorry about my letter.

MOTHER: You're sorry.

RACHEL: Please, Mom. (A beat.) There's something I want you to look at.

MOTHER: Rachel, you and I have a lot to discuss.

RACHEL: It's a book. The Rabbi gave it to me.

> (SHE holds the Talmud out for MOTHER to see.)

It has magical powers.

MOTHER: So this is what you were practicing with the Rabbi? Magic?

RACHEL: If you'd only stop to read a little, maybe you'd understand me.

> (RACHEL tries to hand MOTHER the Talmud. MOTHER pushes it back in Rachel's direction.)

MOTHER: I understand you plenty well.

RACHEL: Please! Open it.

A Talmud Tale

        (RACHEL hands the book to MOTHER, who takes it, but does not open it.)

MOTHER: The Talmud? I don't have time to read.

        (MOTHER tries to hand the book back to RACHEL. RACHEL pushes it back towards her.)

RACHEL: Please!

MOTHER: You're as stubborn as your father.
        (SHE looks at the book.)
I don't know from history. And I don't believe in magic!

        (On the word "magic" SHE opens the book. A magical musical chord strikes.)

RASHI: Elaine?

MOTHER: (stopping in her tracks) Hunh?

RASHI: Elaine Cohen?

        (MOTHER looks all around. Still doesn't "see" him.)

MOTHER: Who's there?

RASHI: (stepping forward to where he can be seen) Let's just say I'm a friend of your daughter.

        (MOTHER sees RASHI and for a moment is frozen with incredulity. SHE can't imagine who it is.)

MOTHER: B-B-Bob?!

RACHEL: No, Mom. Relax! His name's Rashi. And this is Shlomo.

    (SHLOMO steps forward.)

RASHI: My assistant and I were helping Rachel with one of the great stories of the Talmud. Are you familiar with Rakhel and Akiba?

MOTHER: Not really.

RASHI: Not a problem. May I fill you in?

    (HE extends his elbow in a gentlemanly manner.)

MOTHER: Rachel?

RACHEL: (impatient) What?

MOTHER: Is he—

RACHEL: —Yes, he's dead! Only right now, it's as if he's completely alive!

MOTHER: This is what I get for buying you "Harry Potter".

RASHI: Think of this as a temporary journey. You'll be back in no time at all.

SHLOMO: No real time.

RACHEL: Mom, do this for me. Please.

MOTHER: But I have an important meeting with the party planner. We're visiting the zoo! Do you have any idea what's involved in renting a camel?

RASHI: Come with me, and you'll ride one.

RACHEL: Please, Mom?

MOTHER: (acquiescing) Okay.

> (SHE accepts RASHI's arm. RASHI begins to slowly promenade across the stage with MOTHER on his arm, ultimately exiting.)

RASHI: Have you been to Israel?

MOTHER: Ages ago.

RASHI: The year is now 67 C.E., and Akiba, a former shepherd...

> (His voice fades as they continue their conversation. RACHEL stands in disbelief for a moment.)

RACHEL: Just like that?

SHLOMO: He may be lacking in love, but not in charm.
    (A beat.)
May I?

> (SHLOMO extends his elbow in a manner identical to RASHI. RACHEL grabs his arm and both follow RASHI and MOTHER.)

RACHEL: So how is Rakhel? Did she get back with Akiba?

SHLOMO: Not yet. But they've exchanged some letters.

RACHEL: Really? What do the letters say?

SHLOMO: Well, a letter between two people is a very private thing.

(There is a beat as SHLOMO and RACHEL exchange a glance. SHLOMO then eagerly whispers words to a fascinated RACHEL. LIGHTS FADE TO BLACK as they exit.

Scene changes to the Beit Midrash, some "ancient" years later. Several books sit open on the table. AKIBA is holding a letter from RAKHEL. HE has just read a humorous section of it aloud to MEIR. There is a burst of laughter from the two of them.)

MEIR: She has a sharp wit! Almost as sharp as yours!

AKIBA: (affectionately) Ah, she puts me to shame!

MEIR: You are kind to read me her letters, Akiba.

AKIBA: There was a time you had to read them to me!

MEIR: A time long past!
                (dreamily)
So, how does she end it?

AKIBA: She writes:
                (HE reads)
"Waste not a worry. I am content with my life, patiently awaiting the day you are ready." And she signs it, "Your Loving Wife." I am indeed a lucky man.

MEIR: But, what does she mean by that?

AKIBA: By... what?

MEIR: "...the day you are ready." "Ready" for what?

AKIBA: To return. To Jerusalem.

MEIR: To visit your Rakhel.

AKIBA: Not to visit. To live.

MEIR: (horrified) But how could you ever leave the Beit Midrash?!

AKIBA: (defensive) Is it so strange to want to be with my wife? You know she can't live here. But even if she could, I would choose to go back. I wouldn't spend the rest of my life at the study house.

MEIR: You should be so blessed — to live out your days steeped in Torah!

AKIBA: You think I'm not grateful to be here?

MEIR: Then, how could you leave us—abandon the pursuit of Truth?!

AKIBA: Well, maybe I seek a different kind of truth.

MEIR: A fancy excuse!

AKIBA: (persisting) The truth that comes from grasping knowledge and applying it in the world.

MEIR: Knowledge itself has value! It need not be applied.

AKIBA: (heating up) Tell that to the farmer with no crop, who wonders if his sheep should be slaughtered.

MEIR: Where would I meet such a farmer?

AKIBA: My friend, you forget. You are sitting with a shepherd. And what I learn here, I would like to share with others like me.

MEIR: Then let them come and study at the feet of Rabbi Eliezer. You did!

AKIBA: Not everyone can find their way here.

MEIR: (making a joke) Shall we give them a map?

> [Song: "ANYONE CAN!" MUSIC under.]

AKIBA: (stunned into silence for a moment. HE senses something.) Yes! That's right! A "map!" That is exactly what we should give them!

MEIR: The road here may be winding, but surely it's not all that—

AKIBA: —No, no! Not that kind of map.

MEIR: What are you talking about?

AKIBA: (he sings.)

> Why should the Torah
> Be kept from the average man?
> Who gains from Torah?
> Anyone can!
>
> Why should God's teachings
> Be claimed by a privileged clan?
> Who can best learn from them?
> Anyone can!
>
> If we'd open wide the book
> It could be such a blessing!
> Showing people where to look
> For guidance that they need
> Cover worship, farming, food,
> The fine details of dressing
> I'm guessing,
> But they just might feel freed!

A Talmud Tale

> Just as when Moses
> First moved us with God's holy plan,
> We can move mountains
> If anyone can!

MEIR: And what mountain would you have us move? Mount Sinai?!

AKIBA: I am serious, my friend. Just imagine a poor man picking olives on a Friday. Shabbat is coming quickly but he still has much harvesting to do. So, he needs to know how late he is permitted to work. But, when exactly does the Sabbath begin?

MEIR: Well, the Torah has many things to say on that subject—

AKIBA: —But, does he have time to sift through the Torah for his answer? With ten hungry children …and a storm coming?!

MEIR: Well…maybe not—

AKIBA: Now, ….

> (HE holds up his finger for silence.
> For a moment, HE is lost in thought,
> formulating a concept.)

…what if…. he had a book!?

MEIR: What do you mean, "a book?"

AKIBA: (both impatient and excited)
A book! Where all he had to do…. was turn to the section on observing the Sabbath…. call it "Holidays" or "Seasons"…. and there's his answer!

MEIR: But, where is such a book?

AKIBA: (emphatically tapping his own head) Here, my friend!
> (HE points to MEIR's head, as well.)

And here!

            (HE sings)
All through the Torah
Are laws laid since Eden began
List how to find them
So anyone can

MEIR: (trying it on for size)
Anyone can?

AKIBA: Hidden in hist'ry,
Those laws cover quite a wide span
Show how to live them
So anyone can

MEIR: (echoing)
Anyone can!

AKIBA: If we put them into groups
They're easier to follow
Should our people jump through hoops
To simply know what's right?
I say: serve it on a plate,
It's easier to swallow!
And I know,
After a taste, they'll bite!

Life is chaotic
Unless you have faith in a plan
Surely God made one,
And we'll have conveyed one,
That anyone,
Anyone can!

            (HE begins to play-act.)

Say, Farmer!
            (MEIR looks around. HE is confused.)

Yes, you!...With the olive trees?...Shabbat coming?

MEIR: (catching on, after a moment) Oh!...Yes?

AKIBA: Do you have that new book?

MEIR: The book... Why, yes, Neighbor,.... it's right here.

> (HE pulls out imaginary "book." His play-acting is awkward.)

AKIBA: I need to know: shall I plant seeds next year or let my fields lie fallow? What does your book say?

MEIR: It says, well, let me look under—

AKIBA: —"Seeds!"

MEIR: Yes, "Seeds!" That would be a good place to find information. On seeds.

AKIBA: I agree, but wait! Something's come up! We found a dead cockroach in our oven!

MEIR: What a shame!

AKIBA: For the cockroach?

MEIR: For the oven! You'll have to get it purified!

AKIBA: Are you sure?

MEIR: (pointing to a new "spot")
Well, it says so right here. Under... "Purities."

AKIBA: (as himself, for a moment)
"Purities!" Excellent!

MEIR: (gloating a bit)
Sure! Where else would you look for a question on koshering?

AKIBA: (taking him down a peg)
Well, I might look under "Holy Things."

MEIR: (humbled) That's also good.

> (MEIR, suddenly competitive, turns to yet a new "spot.")

Say, have you seen this section yet? "Civil Law and Damages!"

AKIBA: (as "Neighbor," again)
No, but that should help me decide what to do with your wandering goats!

MEIR: My wandering goats?!

AKIBA: They ate the bark off all my trees!

MEIR: (attempting humor) You've got to be....kid-ding!

AKIBA: I am, but all joking aside, what's with that chapter?

MEIR: What?

AKIBA: Look how thick it is!

MEIR: Oh. You mean the one about—

AKIBA: —"Women."
MEIR: Yes. (HE chuckles.) It should be its own book!

AKIBA: And I see you're having trouble with your wife.

MEIR: What makes you say that?

A Talmud Tale

AKIBA: The pages are practically falling out.

MEIR: Oh. Just a little research.

   (THEY laugh together. AKIBA sings.)

AKIBA: (sings)
   If we'd open wide the book

MEIR: It could be so exciting!

AKIBA: Showing people where to look

MEIR: For when it's prime to pray.

AKIBA: Like a lantern in a storm

BOTH: The darkness we'd be lighting

AKIBA: Igniting

BOTH: Something as bright as day!

   Why can't the Torah
   Be used by the average man?
   We'll spread the Torah
   From S'fat to Gomorrah
   So anyone, anyone can!
   Anyone, anyone can!

[End of song.]

   (THEY exit, arm in arm. RASHI, MOTHER, RACHEL, and SHLOMO emerge from the wings. MOTHER separates herself from the rest, and goes looking around inquisitively. SHE becomes increasingly agitated during the following:)

RASHI: And so, in the months and years to come, Akiba and Meir continued to give shape to their ideas—

SHLOMO: —and others joined in—

RASHI: —Yes, until they settled on the six sections that, to this day, comprise the Mishnah, half of the modern Talmud.

SHLOMO: Gemara is the other half.

RACHEL: I get it. Akiba's not just in this book, he wrote it!

RASHI: Well, he began it. Then, people like me come along, and it keeps growing and growing and is something the matter?..Mrs. Cohen!

MOTHER: What happened to the table? And the chairs?

RACHEL: Mom!

RASHI: They're gone. We've left the Beit Midrash.

MOTHER: So you can just pick up and go anywhere you want?

RASHI: Well...

SHLOMO: We go wherever Rachel leads us.

MOTHER: I see. Then...
    (grabbing Rachel's arm)
...lead me home!

RACHEL: No! I have to see Rakhel. You have to see her!

MOTHER: Why? Do I really need to see the poor girl practically starve herself so her husband can bury his nose in a book? Yet once again, the woman is less important!

RASHI: She's not starving.

MOTHER: You told me she sacrificed a life of guaranteed comfort.

RASHI: Yes, but—

RACHEL: (to SHLOMO) —I knew this was a bad idea!

MOTHER: (to RASHI)
Mr. Rashi, I mean no disrespect, but from my point of view, the wife gives up everything so the man can go dabble in philosophy. There's a word for their relationship, but it's not "marriage"!

RACHEL: As usual, Mom, you've missed the point. First of all, Akiba's not dabbling! He's the real deal! And second, Rakhel doesn't care about "comfort". If it was "comfort" she was after, she could have had any wealthy man she wanted. But she rejected all of them.

    (with difficulty)

She's following her heart!

    (Pause.)

SHLOMO: Rakhel is indeed an impressive woman, Mrs. Cohen. Not unlike yourself.

    (RACHEL's eyes widen; SHLOMO
    motions to her to back down.)
You might be surprised.

MOTHER: Alright. This I gotta see.

RASHI: Rachel, your mother's not the only one questioning the choice

Rakhel has made.

RACHEL: How so?

RASHI: There are others, of all walks, who are wondering how long she can—

SHLOMO: —Rash!

RASHI: Yes, I shouldn't spoil it. Come!

>(ALL exit. Scene shifts to a small shop. RAKHEL is working at a spinning wheel, humming contentedly. SHE is surrounded by baskets filled with skeins of spun and dyed wool. A well dressed, haughty woman, MARTA BAT BAITUSI, appears in the doorway. The "Moderns" appear in the shadows, observing the scene.)

MARTA: Shalom, Rakhel.

RAKHEL: Marta, what a surprise!

MARTA: Are you open for business?

RAKHEL: I have never known you to do your own shopping.

MARTA: I wanted to see how you were doing.

RAKHEL: Never better.

MARTA: (looking around) You needn't put up a front, Rakhel. I do have eyes.

RAKHEL: (sharply) And a tongue!
>(There is an uncomfortable silence.)

RAKHEL: (continued) I'm sorry. That was unkind.

MARTA: And I'm sorry you feel that my concern merits mockery!

RAKHEL: You didn't deserve that. (Pause) Now, what can I get for you? I have yarns of many colors.

MARTA: Why don't you give me... five skeins of each. I know how hard you must struggle to feed yourself.

> (RAKHEL restrains herself from reacting,
> as SHE begins to collect the wool.)

You know, Rakhel, I have made some inquiries...and Rabban Gamliel says that this... marriage of yours... did not really "take." It could easily be annulled. After all, the shepherd abandoned you right after the wedding—if you can call it a wedding without a single witness.

RAKHEL: God was our witness.

> (MUSIC under: "A CROWN OF STRAW")

And my husband did not "abandon" me. He went—with my blessing—to study Torah.

MARTA: Your blessing perhaps, but not your father's.

RAKHEL: He sent you!

MARTA: You know you can still restore your family's honor.

RAKHEL: And he can come and tell me that himself.

MARTA: Your father is in great despair... if you care to know.

RAKHEL: I've tried to visit him. He won't see me.

MARTA: Can you blame the man? You've humiliated him!

RAKHEL: (flabbergasted) I've—?! How? By marrying a great soul?

MARTA: A shepherd!? You could have had anyone! A house with gardens! And servants! Instead… look at this life you're condemned to!

RAKHEL: Not "condemned!"

    (SHE sings)

    [song: "NOT ANOTHER MAN (Reprise)"]

    Not another way can I imagine spending time
    Knowing that Akiba is a scholar now, means I'm contented

    Many other men
    Might offer comfort and ease
    Promising a life
    Where I could do as I please

    But would such living please me?
    Could such comfort do?
    When you find a man so true…

    (RAKHEL hands MARTA a basket full
    of yarns she has selected.)

MARTA: I don't begin to understand, Rakhel.

    (SHE hands RAKHEL three large purses
    filled with coins.)

Here…will this be enough?

RAKHEL: (returning all but one of them) I don't need your charity, Marta.

MARTA: (shaking her head) You need a lot more than that.

(MARTA leaves.)

RAKHEL: (throws down the purse of coins)
Tell me I'm romantic
As I tell you true
Not another man will do
Not another man, but you!

(RACHEL and MOTHER step forward to examine RAKHEL more closely; RASHI and SHLOMO follow behind. RAKHEL disappears. There is an awkward pause as RACHEL stares at her MOTHER.)

RACHEL: So?

MOTHER: It all makes sense.

RACHEL: You see, she is so amazing! Thank you, Mom. I know you really didn't want to come here, but aren't you glad now that you—

MOTHER: —It makes sense that you would be so affected by the girl's story.

RACHEL: Hunh?

MOTHER: The brashness, the flying in the face of common sense—
RACHEL: —wait, wait, wait! Are you saying Rakhel should have agreed to dump him?!

MOTHER: No, I'm just saying that I can see how you would think that Rakhel would be right to reject the annulment.

RACHEL: And you think she was wrong?
MOTHER: You want to know what I think? I think she's crazy—giving up

her own future so she can slave for a man?! It's pathetic. And she clearly doesn't think how her poor father must feel. Imagine, raising a fine young woman—and so wonderfully attractive—and what does the daughter do? Turns her father into the laughingstock of the community. No, Rakhel is no angel. She is as self-deluding and flawed a human being as they come. And that, my precious angel, is what I think!

>   (A short pause. RACHEL stews over what
>   MOTHER has just said.)

RASHI: I can see we may have a difference of opinion.

RACHEL: (angrily, almost shaking with emotion)
So Mom, you don't believe in True Love?

MOTHER: (caustic)
It's not true love, it's spite! Rakhel was spoiled rotten and now she's spiteful!

RACHEL: (screaming) Ahhhh! How can you say that?

MOTHER: I just did.

RACHEL: (Taking an aggressive step towards her mother, RACHEL makes a threatening gesture as she is about to say the word "you"):
I — hate —

>   (A magical musical chord strikes, and
>   RACHEL freezes in position, as does
>   MOTHER, in a defensive posture that is
>   oddly comical, all simultaneously with):

RASHI: (singing a loud "cantorial" riff)
AH—————————-
>   (MUSIC under.)

SHLOMO: Cutting it a teeny bit close, wouldn't you say?
RASHI: Close is good. They both got to let off steam.

SHLOMO: (with pad in hand, "ready-to-go") My pencil is sharp.

RASHI: I haven't found the words yet.

SHLOMO: I love it when you're pushed to your oratorical limits.

RASHI: Well, I may need back-up on this one. Okay, let 'er rip!

> (With a hand motion from SHLOMO, RACHEL is "unfrozen" and finishes her sentence. MOTHER remains "frozen" in her stance throughout the entire song.)

RACHEL: —YOU! (SHE notices her MOTHER is still "frozen.") What's happening?! (SHE turns to RASHI) Tell me what's happening!

RASHI: Standard policy: "No Train Wrecks Allowed!"

> (RACHEL waves her hand in front of her MOTHER's face and gets no reaction.)

RACHEL: I see. This is kind of like: "Situation normal!" Nothing gets through! You don't know how that feels!

RASHI: Oh yes, Rachel, I think I do. And I suspect I'm not alone.
> (HE gestures towards other ANCIENTS as THEY appear. HE sings.)

[Song: "OLD AS TIME"]

There's a voice inside of you
A voice that's ancient as it's new
Crying: "Tell her, how she treats you is a crime!"
And this longing to reveal
Ev'ry hurt you feel
Is a longing that is old as time

>   Old as time
>   Old as time
>   I know that I'm not the first to say
>   That however much you rage
>   You cannot escape your age
>   Yet with patience, you will make your way

RACHEL: **But, it's hard to keep track of where I'm supposed to be going!**

RASHI: (sympathetic) **I know. I know.**

FIRST FEMALE ANCIENT:
>   There's a choice at every turn

SECOND FEMALE ANCIENT:
>   You learn to take the time to choose

BOTH & MALE ANCIENT:
>   And you stumble, even when you're in your prime

AKIBA & RAKHEL:
>   There are chances that you take
>   With each choice you make

ALL OF THE ABOVE:
>   Needing courage that is old as time

RASHI (backed by ENSEMBLE):
>   Old as time
>   Old as time
>   I know I won't be the last to say
>   That whenever you feel lost,
>   Unmoored and tempest-tossed,
>   If you sail on, God will light your way

THREE FEMALE ANCIENTS:
> You question: Are your parents really on your side?

THREE OR MORE MALE ANCIENTS:
> Are teachers there to test you or to teach?

ENSEMBLE:
> Adults might undervalue what you hold with pride
> And compromise seems ever out of reach

RASHI: You're not alone in all of this
> For truth be told...,

RASHI, AKIBA, RAKHEL, BEN KALBA SAVUA:
> We all at some point wonder

BEN KALBA SAVUA:
> And wondering itself is old as time

RACHEL: That's right! The Bible says to honor your parents, but what if they don't honor you... and what you think is important?!

(SHE drops her head, moping.)

RASHI: Growing up can be like walking a tightrope— it's best if you look ahead... (HE lifts her chin)... not down!

ALL:
> Old as time
> Old as time
> I know that I'm not the first to say
> That whatever path you take
> Whatever mold you break,

RAKHEL: If you hold on

AKIBA: And keep searching

BOTH & RABBI ELIEZER:
    And stay faithful

RASHI: B'ezrat Hashem

RASHI, AKIBA, RAKHEL, RABBI ELIEZER, FEMALE ANCIENT:
    You can find your way

ALL:
    And you will

RASHI: I know you will

ALL:
    Someday!

    [End of song.]

    (The sound of thunder, followed by distant rain. All ANCIENTS except RASHI and SHLOMO exit quickly.)

SHLOMO: Could be a storm coming.

RACHEL: Well, thanks, Rashi. I feel so much better.

RASHI: Good. Quickly now, I can't keep your mother suspended forever.

    (HE signals SHLOMO.)

RACHEL: What do I do?

    (SHLOMO helps RACHEL move back to the position she was in when she was about to finish the sentence "I hate you".)

RASHI: In a moment, your mom will snap back to life. You'll pick up the conversation with her exactly where you left off. Okay?

RACHEL: You mean?!—

RASHI: —Don't worry, you'll find the right words.

RACHEL: Stop saying that!

> (A magical musical chord strikes. MOTHER "snaps" back to life. RASHI and SHLOMO retreat a bit. MUSIC under.)

MOTHER: Wha? Where? What were you saying?

RACHEL: I... ha.. (SHE cannot bring herself to say the word "hate.")

MOTHER: Yes?

RACHEL: I... ha..

MOTHER: Say it.
> (MUSIC out.)

RACHEL: I... have an idea.

MOTHER: Hunh?

RACHEL: Uh, yes, I've been thinking. Wouldn't it be better if we could both just, "sail on?"

MOTHER:: Wha?!

RACHEL: (mimicking RASHI's previous gesture during "OLD AS TIME")
"Sail on."

(MOTHER mimics RACHEL's gesture, but is still confused.)

RASHI: Uh, Rachel's trying to tell you that—

RACHEL: (quickly, half-embarrassed) —we shouldn't give up on each other.

MOTHER: Oh.

(MOTHER repeats the "sail on" gesture.)

"Sail on." Okay. As long as it's a two-way ocean.

(The sound of thunder fades away.)

SHLOMO: Hey, the sun just pierced the clouds!

RASHI: Baruch HaShem! Come, there's another storm elsewhere, but it's the kind none of us can afford to miss!

(The MUSIC of "OLD AS TIME" wells up as RASHI escorts the others off. RACHEL is the last to exit. SHE turns to observe a single spotlight which represents the sun. SHE feels empowered.

FADE TO BLACK.
Scene changes to the Beit Midrash. AKIBA and RABBI ELIEZER appear to be in the midst of an argument.)

RABBI ELIEZER: So, this is all about the wife, then?

AKIBA: Not just the wife. But yes, I want to see my Rakhel.

RABBI ELIEZER: And for that you would not only leave us for good, but take with you nearly all of my best students?

AKIBA: They are choosing to go.

RABBI ELIEZER: I find that hard to—

AKIBA: But some have sworn they will return here, as soon as they have been with me in Jerusalem—

RABBI ELIEZER: Nonsense!

> (HE slams his fist down loudly on a table.
> There is a tense pause.)

AKIBA: Look, I know how you must feel. When I was a shepherd, every so often I would have to say goodbye to part of my flock. And that wasn't so easy. Thanks to you, I am no longer a shepherd, and now, I, Meir, your other students—the ones who are going—feel as though we are being called away. Pulled by a power so undeniable we are compelled to either let ourselves be swept up in it, or hide our heads and pretend that the power does not exist. But it does exist!

RABBI ELIEZER: Don't tell me this is God's doing!

AKIBA: I can't say who or what is responsible. I only know that the ideas that Meir and I began discussing months ago and which have preoccupied so many minds, and dominated so many discussions here—

RABBI ELIEZER: —to the exclusion of real study!

AKIBA: (inflamed) Oh, but how can you say what is "real study" and what is not? Is the study any less "real" if concerned men are debating how Torah can have meaning and purpose for real people in real life?

> (A silence.)

RABBI ELIEZER: (He has heard.) I guess, like everything else, even the issue of what makes study "real" has more than one side.

> (HE sings.)
> [Song: "BOTH SIDES OF AN ISSUE (Reprise)"]

> The day I took you in
> I never would have guessed
> The shepherd who could barely read
> Would soon lead all the rest

AKIBA: Oh, how the tables turn

BOTH: Just look at us today

RABBI ELIEZER::
> You, intent on leaving

AKIBA: You, entreating me to stay!

RABBI ELIEZER: I guess this is what the Almighty might call one of Life's little ironies.
> (Suddenly serious.)
You'll leave behind a great hole.

AKIBA: It was you who turned my mind into a shovel. And taught me how to dig.

BOTH:
> Seeing both sides of an issue
> Can be painful for a friend

AKIBA:
> When one sees a new beginning

RABBI ELIEZER:
> While the other sees an end

BOTH:
    Though these partners now are parting
    At a place we don't agree
    When you're gone
    You'll still live on
    Inside of me

        (A clarinet continues the plaintive melody under.)

AKIBA: (extending his hand) Well, I should go now, Rabbi—

RABBI ELIEZER: (interrupting) Please, call me Eliezer.

AKIBA: (touched) "Eliezer." It has truly been an—

RABBI ELIEZER: (dignifying AKIBA for the first time with the title...) —No, "Rabbi" Akiba... the honor has been mine!

        (THEY shake... then hug.)
        [End of song.]

        (BLACKOUT. RABBI ELIEZER and AKIBA exit. RASHI, SHLOMO, RACHEL and MOTHER enter.)

RASHI: And from that moment on, Akiba-the-shepherd became Rabbi Akiba to all those who knew him.

SHLOMO: And even those who didn't.

MOTHER: What happens now?

RASHI: They will head to Jerusalem. Rabbi Akiba, that is, and hundreds of disciples.

SHLOMO: Thousands.

RACHEL: And we get to go. Right?

RASHI: Yes, but there are two ways to go. One, as dispassionate observers.

SHLOMO: The other, as passionate participants.

RASHI: The two of you must choose: either the first way?

SHLOMO: Or the second.

> (RASHI places his hand on RACHEL's shoulder and gently nudges her towards MOTHER.)

RASHI: Choose. Together.

> (MUSIC under. RASHI and SHLOMO take a step back. RACHEL and MOTHER eye each other uncomfortably for a moment.)

MOTHER: Uh, we're better off watching.

RACHEL: No, Mom. Look, it's really fun! You get to talk with ancient people. And when it's over, it's like nobody knows you were even there!

> (RABBI AKIBA enters wearing a colorful new robe. He is followed by a weary MEIR. In mime, they carry on a heated conversation. One or two weary OTHERS trail MEIR. They are all carrying bags.)

MOTHER: And that's how I prefer to be. Invisible!

RACHEL: (seeing AKIBA and MEIR)
Look! You see them there? You can't tell me you wouldn't like to just walk over and strike up a conversation with them, could you?

A Talmud Tale

(RACHEL starts to pull a reluctant MOTHER closer to AKIBA.)

MOTHER: Please, I'm wearing high heels!

RACHEL: Come on!

(SHLOMO thinks to stop RACHEL, but RASHI motions to him to "let her learn for herself".)

RACHEL: Ahem! Rabbi Akiba? Rabbi Akiba?

RABBI AKIBA: (to MEIR) Wait!

MEIR: What is it?

RABBI AKIBA: I thought I heard something.

MEIR: You're always hearing voices. It's probably God trying to convince you that we all have got to stop and set up camp for the night!

(Pause.)

RABBI AKIBA: Right.

(Clearly exhausted, MEIR slings his bag off his shoulder and eagerly sits down. HE signals OTHERS to sit. MEIR pulls out a gourd from his bag and drinks water. HE pours a little water on his face. RABBI AKIBA remains standing. HE is lost in thought.)

MOTHER: You see? He doesn't like us.

RACHEL: He doesn't see us!

RASHI: I'm afraid it will be difficult to engage Akiba in conversation just now.

RACHEL: Why?

    [Song: "UP TO YOU (Reprise)"]

    (RABBI AKIBA begins humming a melody. He takes a notebook out and makes some notes for an upcoming speech.)

RASHI: Rabbi Akiba has a great deal on his mind. His legion of followers is growing. Word of the human caravan is spreading throughout the countryside. A large crowd is rumored to be congregating in Jerusalem to greet him. What will he say to the gathered masses?

RABBI AKIBA:

    (HE sings introspectively; MEIR and OTHERS are oblivious:)

Up to you
It is always up to you
What you say
And what you do
Is up to you

    (MUSIC under. As AKIBA hums, he is joined by offstage VOICES.)

RASHI: And when he finally sees Rakhel, what will he do?

SHLOMO: And what of Ben Kalba Savua?

RASHI: What will Akiba say to him?

SHLOMO: What will he say to Akiba?

RACHEL: (overloaded) So many questions!

RASHI: The only way to get through to Akiba now would be for you to join the throng!

MOTHER: Hold on now! Throng, shmong!! I am not going to let my daughter go off and get squashed among the raucous, unwashed, ancient masses! Even if they are Jewish.

RACHEL: This is a once-in-a-lifetime opportunity for me! For us!

RASHI: Rachel cannot go unless you go, too, Mrs. Cohen. That's the deal.

MOTHER: So you're saying it's either the front row or the skybox?

RABBI AKIBA and RASHI:
    Wisely choose
    Will you gain or will you lose?

ANCIENT CHORUS joins in:
    Can you put yourself in someone else's shoes—?

MOTHER: ('enough already!')
—I'll do it, I'll do it!
        (SHE removes her high heels.)

RACHEL: You will, Mom? "Join the throng"?

MOTHER: Gotta give the heels a rest some time.

    (RACHEL gives MOTHER a hug.)

RASHI: Ladies, no time to dawdle. Much to prepare! Come!

    (RASHI exits briskly. RACHEL follows. SHLOMO whispers to MOTHER his ideas on a change of wardrobe for her as they exit together. The last strain of "UP TO YOU" plays as AKIBA puts his notebook away, sits down next to MEIR, and falls asleep with the OTHERS as LIGHTS FADE to BLACK. MUSIC under.

At rise, BEN KALBA SAVUA is seated in a throne-like chair in his home. Standing to one side, ORNA, a female servant, pours him wine from a copper carafe.)

KALBA SAVUA: Is it sweet?

ORNA: Yes, of course.
  (SHE hands him a goblet.)
The one you always like.

  (HE drinks. BEN DAVID enters unannounced. Seeing the servant, BEN DAVID appears anxious. MUSIC out.)

BEN DAVID: Oh, pardon me. Perhaps I should come back—

KALBA SAVUA: —No, please! Stay! Would you care for some wine? Orna! (He beckons her.)

BEN DAVID: No thank you.

KALBA SAVUA: Well? What brings you?

BEN DAVID: About tomorrow.

KALBA SAVUA: Ah, yes.

BEN DAVID: Have you come to a decision?

KALBA SAVUA: (mockingly) On the visit of the "Great Rabbi"?
  (HE sips more wine.)
I will go. If only out of curiosity.

BEN DAVID: **And?**

> (HE affects a cough; KALBA SAVUA
> appears not to understand; BEN DAVID
> leans in and whispers:)

What about the servants? May they go?

KALBA SAVUA: **No need to whisper, Ben David.**
> (loudly)

All my staff may attend!
> (HE signals ORNA. BEN DAVID and
> ORNA seem enthusiastic.)

Why should they miss an opportunity to experience a false prophet?

> (HE hands ORNA the depleted goblet.)

We all have to drink from the cup of disenchantment.

> (BEN DAVID and ORNA eye each other
> despairingly. BLACKOUT.
>
> SPOTLIGHT up on a corner where
> RABBI AKIBA has just handed
> MESSENGER a letter.)

RABBI AKIBA: **It's a small yarn shop.** Make sure to give it to her when there's no one else around. I don't want word to get back to her father. Not just yet.

MESSENGER: **B'seder.** (In Hebrew, b'seder means "okay")

> (HE/SHE goes. LIGHTS UP to full
> revealing RABBI AKIBA beside a
> string of followers including MEIR and
> OTHERS on a tree-lined road.)

RABBI AKIBA: (loudly) Now, my friends, are you ready for another chorus?

> (Some impromptu reaction from the OTHERS. ALL begin to march jauntily as they sing a capella):

RABBI AKIBA:	MEIR and OTHERS:
A SIMPLE SHAWL	
	A SIMPLE SHAWL
A SIMPLE SHAWL	
	A SIMPLE SHAWL
MORE GORGEOUS THAN THE ROYAL ROBES OF SOLOMON AND SAUL	
	SOLOMON AND—

POOR WOMAN ON ROAD: (appearing suddenly from behind a tree) I have a simple shawl! It is tattered and torn, but just big enough to cover both of us as we lay at night.

> (The WOMAN's young SON emerges from behind her. AKIBA and OTHERS have stopped in their tracks.)

RABBI AKIBA: You needn't own a shawl, or anything, Madam, to march in our parade.

WOMAN: So you're Rabbi Akiba?

RABBI AKIBA: I am.

WOMAN: May we join you?

RABBI AKIBA: Of course. Take any place in line. Would you like some food? Give them food, please!

> (The WOMAN and SON move behind MEIR and OTHERS as RABBI AKIBA resumes:)

Though wealthy men wear linen
While wailing at the wall

> (RACHEL and MOTHER suddenly appear roadside. THEY are in ancient garb, but relatively well-dressed, both with elegant shawls.)

RACHEL: (jumping out)
I have a simple shawl.

MOTHER:
I have a simple shawl.

> (RABBI AKIBA does a double-take.)

RABBI AKIBA:
Why, our song has been heard throughout the land, then? Yes?

RACHEL: Oh, yes. We heard it from.. way yonder!

RABBI AKIBA: Do I know you? What village would you be from?

RACHEL: Village? Oh, well, you could say I'm from a village, but that's not how—

RABBI AKIBA: —From where then?

MOTHER: She's from Greenwich Village*. (*Her answer can match the actual location where the musical is being performed.)

RACHEL: Oh, this is my mom... uh... my mother.

MOTHER: A pleasure.

RABBI AKIBA: Greenwich Village? Hmm, I once knew all the towns on the outskirts of Jerusalem.

MOTHER: It's a new one.

RABBI AKIBA: That would explain it. Care to join us? We will be entering the city square tomorrow at noon.

MOTHER: Certainly.

RABBI AKIBA: And if you wouldn't mind, I'd like the two of you at my side. Let all Jerusalem see that our followers come from near as well as far.

RACHEL and MOTHER: Okay.

RABBI AKIBA: (for all to hear) Friends, let your voices be heard echoing from here to-? (HE looks at MOTHER.)

MOTHER: Greenwich Village.

RABBI AKIBA: Greenwich Village!

> (As ALL sing again, they exit, marching. We observe that RASHI and SHLOMO have inconspicuously blended in.)

RABBI AKIBA:	ALL OTHERS:
A simple shawl	
A simple shawl	
A simple shawl	
	A simple shawl
More gorgeous than the	
Royal robes of Solomon and Saul	
	Solomon and Saul
Though wealthy men wear linen	
While wailing at the wall	
When called to prayer	When called to prayer
I would rather wear	I would rather wear
A simple shawl	A simple shawl

(MUSIC continues. AKIBA and his followers vanish as RAKHEL appears on another part of the stage, alone in her yarn shop. SHE has just finished reading the letter RABBI AKIBA has sent ahead.)

RAKHEL: **At last!!**

SHE reaches into a special hiding place and pulls out the "crown of straw" that AKIBA had made for her years before. Singing the melody wordlessly, SHE places the "crown of straw" on her head, and begins to dance around the shop, clutching the letter to her breast. As SHE does so, MARTA BAT BAITUSI returns to the shop. SHE watches RAKHEL incredulously for a moment.)

MARTA: **Have you lost your senses along with everything else?!**

RAKHEL: (looking up, smiling): **So it would seem!**

(MARTA stands awkwardly for a moment, unsure of how to interpret RAKHEL's mood.)

MARTA: **Well...I have what I hope will be good news.**

RAKHEL: **(stops dancing) More?**

MARTA: (ignoring her)
When I told your father how dire your circumstances were, he agreed to take pity and help you out with a small stipend—

(RAKHEL is too ecstatic about her husband's imminent return to take offense.)

RAKHEL: (interrupting)
—Marta, I now see that under it all, you really do mean well.

MARTA: I imagine that was meant as a compliment. I would think your father's generosity might give you some actual cause for dancing.

RAKHEL: Oh, I already have cause!

MARTA: Oh?

RAKHEL: (almost mischievously): Have you not heard? There's a great rabbi coming to Jerusalem! He will speak by the Western Wall this very day.

MARTA: If I thought the orations of some rabbi could fill one's belly, I would understand your glee—!

>   (RAKHEL grabs MARTA's hands and starts spinning her around.)

RAKHEL: —Oh, Marta, Marta! Come with me, and you will understand!

>   (SHE releases MARTA, grabs her own "simple shawl," then, threading her arm through MARTA's again, escorts her out the door. The shop disappears, and the two women join others gathered in the streets of Jerusalem to hear RABBI AKIBA speak. As the scene opens, AKIBA is addressing the throng which includes RACHEL and MOTHER. There is a great burst of laughter from the crowd. His good natured humor is winning them over.)

CROWD MEMBER: (shouting merrily)
No one told us the Great Rabbi was also a jokester!

RABBI AKIBA: Laughter opens the heart, my friends...and the ears! And now, a parable: One night, our blessed patriarch, Jacob, having fled into exile from his father's wrath, lay down, exhausted, in the wilderness. Nothing but a hard stone could he find for a pillow. But, so tired was he, no sooner did he rest his head, than he began to dream. He dreamed of a magnificent ladder, connecting earth to heaven and heaven to earth.

RACHEL: (aside, whispering) Mom, it's my Torah portion!

MOTHER: (drawn into RABBI AKIBA's story) Shh!

RABBI AKIBA: I, too, had a dream—of another sort of ladder...one that also connects earth to heaven. And as a good ladder should, it will help anyone who needs a little leg up. When you climb it, and look back down, you will be able to see the very earth you tread upon every day, with just a little more perspective. And the higher you climb, the more you understand how your life on earth may be led.

CROWD MEMBER: Where can we find this "ladder?"

MEIR: (excitedly) It is a book! Of study!

BEN DAVID: A book?!
RABBI AKIBA: My friend speaks true. This "ladder" will come to be called the Talmud.

> (AKIBA reveals a shiny book that he had been concealing.)

MARTA: But we already have five holy books. Why do we need another?

RABBI AKIBA: Why? (HE laughs.) Thank you for asking! Why is the act of interpreting the holy books left only to the scholars?

> (Some hubbub among the CROWD.)

KALBA SAVUA: (loudly) Because you can see what we do not.

> (Hushed silence in the CROWD.)

Or so we're told.

RABBI AKIBA: (holding up the book) Yes, but with this "ladder" anyone can see as far as the eye will take them.

[Song: "ANYONE CAN (Reprise)"]

MEIR: **Anyone!**

KALBA SAVUA: **Anyone?!**

RABBI AKIBA: (sings)
> Why should the Torah
> Be kept from the average man?
> Who gains from Torah?

MEIR and RABBI AKIBA:
> Anyone can!

RABBI AKIBA:
> Why should God's teachings
> Be claimed by a privileged clan?
> Who can best learn from them?

MEIR, 2 OTHERS (MALE), AKIBA:
> Anyone can!

MEIR, 2 OTHERS:
> Having problems on the farm?

RABBI AKIBA (pointing to a page in the book):
> A practical solution!

MEIR, 2 OTHERS:
> If a neighbor does you harm?

RABBI AKIBA:
> A way to make amends

MEIR, 2 OTHERS:
>If your cow's not giving milk?

RABBI AKIBA:
>You find a substitution.

MEIR: (shouting joyfully)
>It's a revolution!

RABBI AKIBA, MEIR, 2 OTHERS:
>Only we all stay friends!
>
>Deep in the Torah
>Are laws laid when Eden began
>We've demystified them—
>Revealed them and tried them—
>Now anyone,
>Anyone can!

>(KALBA SAVUA steps out of the crowd)

KALBA SAVUA: **Rabbi!**

RACHEL: (whispering to her MOTHER)
That's Rakhel's father!

MOTHER: (finding him appealing)
Very nice!

>(KALBA SAVUA takes the Talmud book and reacts to how thick it is.)

KALBA SAVUA: This is an awfully big "ladder!" Aren't you afraid people may fall?!

RABBI AKIBA: People may...but the "ladder" won't! So, you can always climb back up.

(RABBI AKIBA retrieves the book and walks through the CROWD, exhibiting it. CROWD MEMBERS come forward to ask/sing questions:)

CROWD MEMBER:
If I can't erase a debt?

RABBI AKIBA: (thumbing to a section)
There're many ways to pay it!

SECOND CROWD MEMBER:
If I need to get a "get?"

RABBI AKIBA: (pointing to the book)
A method to employ.

SEVERAL CROWD MEMBERS:
If I want to thank the Lord?

RABBI AKIBA:
A thousand ways to say it!

(add MEIR and TWO MEN)
Display it!

(THEY joyfully raise their hands in praise toward heaven.)

Living each day with joy!

Just as when Moses
First moved us with God's holy plan,

RABBI AKIBA:
(HE opens his arms to encompass the whole CROWD.)

We can move mountains!

ALL FOUR MEN:
'Cause anyone can!

RABBI AKIBA: (enlisting individuals in the CROWD.)
Anyone can!

FEMALE CROWD MEMBER:
Anyone can!

RABBI AKIBA:
Anyone can!

FEMALE AND MALE CROWD MEMBER:
Anyone can!

RABBI AKIBA:
Anyone can!

SEVERAL CROWD MEMBERS:
Anyone can!

RABBI AKIBA:
Anyone can!

ALL (except RABBI AKIBA):
Anyone can, anyone can!

>(Short musical interlude during which the CROWD puts RABBI AKIBA in a chair and lifts him above their heads.)

ALL (with RABBI AKIBA):
Anyone, anyone can!

>[End of song.]

KALBA SAVUA: (stepping forward again)
So tell me, Rabbi. Does this Talmud of yours address how a father can ever forgive a daughter who has disgraced him in the eyes of the world?

RABBI AKIBA: (motioning the CROWD to lower him down)
And how did this daughter do such a thing?

KALBA SAVUA: By marrying a man who could never bring honor to her family name. She could have wed anyone in the land, rich man or scholar. But instead, she chose an ignorant shepherd.

RABBI AKIBA: And where is she now? This daughter... with her ignorant shepherd?

(RAKHEL steps out of the CROWD. SHE is wearing the "crown of straw.")
RAKHEL: She has come, with pride...

> [MUSIC under, quietly: "A CROWN OF STRAW"]

...to welcome the Great Rabbi back to Jerusalem!

> (Her eyes meet AKIBA's. THEY are absolutely still for a moment, drinking each other in. Then, AKIBA smiles broadly and RAKHEL moves swiftly forward to embrace him. KALBA SAVUA is stunned to see her, and embarrassed by her apparent disrespect towards the Rabbi.)

KALBA SAVUA: Rakhel!
> (A MALE FOLLOWER steps forward, between RAKHEL and RABBI AKIBA.)

MALE FOLLOWER: Woman!
> (HE intercepts RAKHEL.)

A Talmud Tale

Show the Rabbi some respect!

> (RABBI AKIBA moves to the
> FOLLOWER and gently frees RAKHEL
> from his grasp.)

RABBI AKIBA: No, my friend. It is she who deserves respect. For everything I am, or have to give, is thanks to her.

RAKHEL: (Turns to KALBA SAVUA) Father, don't you recognize your shepherd?

> (KALBA SAVUA's face registers the truth.
> HE falls to his knees and begins to sob.)

KALBA SAVUA: (to RAKHEL) Forgive me! (HE turns his face to RABBI AKIBA) Forgive me, Rabbi!

> (RABBI AKIBA helps him up.)

RABBI AKIBA: (gently) Father.

> (KALBA SAVUA regains his composure
> and turns to the CROWD.)

KALBA SAVUA: (proudly pointing) My son-in-law!

RAKHEL: (to AKIBA) My husband.

RABBI AKIBA: (tenderly taking her hand) My wife.

MOTHER: My God! (SHE chokes back tears.)
> (The CROWD surges forward to get a
> closer look.)

MEIR: Make room, everyone, please! A little privacy for the couple!

> (The CROWD steps back. A magical

musical chord strikes, as RASHI steps forward. The CROWD then disappears. Remaining on stage are RASHI, SHLOMO, MEIR, RABBI AKIBA, RAKHEL, RACHEL, MOTHER and BEN KALBA SAVUA. RABBI AKIBA and RAKHEL are holding hands, gazing at each other lovingly.)

RASHI: Excuse me, Rabbi. May we have a brief word with you?

MEIR: Sir—

RABBI AKIBA: —Let him speak.

RASHI: Rabbi, we have come a long distance to be with you at this moment. In fact, we have traveled across centuries.

RABBI AKIBA: (extremely intrigued) Aha! (Deja vu) Haven't you come before?

RACHEL: (excited to be remembered) Yes! At the study house.

RASHI: When you were first learning Torah.

RABBI AKIBA: Of course! I remember! (To RACHEL) That's how I knew you!

RASHI: And we are all returning shortly to our respective homes. When Rachel returns, she will be entering adulthood through a distinctly modern ritual known as the bat mitzvah. Do you have any advice for her?
RABBI AKIBA: Adulthood? Enter slowly!

(The ADULTS laugh.)

RASHI: But, there's more — unlike her daughter, Rachel's mother feels the bat mitzvah ought to include a lavish party, complete with a king's feast, dancing, and camels. What advice would you have for her?

RABBI AKIBA: Stay away from camels!

> (ANCIENTS laugh.)

RASHI: (frustrated by the flipness of RABBI AKIBA's answers): Hmm.

MEIR: (to RASHI) Are you finished?

RABBI AKIBA: (waving MEIR off) Meir!...Now, we have, on the one hand, Rachel and her mother, and, on the other, Rakhel and her father. My shepherd's instincts are telling me that they are all of the same flock.

RASHI: Yes, exactly!

MOTHER: Wait a minute! I am not a sheep!

AKIBA: Of course you're not. It's just that I still keep an eye out... when I notice some dear ones are straying too far apart.

> [Song: "HALFWAY." MUSIC under.]

RASHI: Oh, I think they're all well on their way back together.

BEN KALBA SAVUA:
(understanding, and stepping towards RAKHEL)
And it isn't as far as I feared.

> (HE spreads his arms towards RAKHEL, beckoning her to hug him. SHE takes a few steps away from him. There is a moment of discomfort between them. Her back is half-turned away from him as HE lets his arms down and sings.)

I tried to listen

Couldn't always hear you
Had some sort of fear
You had too much to say
Crazy to be frightened
But sometimes we don't see
The picture, complete
The honey, so sweet
But look! We can meet
Halfway

RAKHEL: RACHEL:
(to KALBA SAVUA)   (to her MOTHER)
I tried to tell you   I tried to tell you
Couldn't say it nicely   Couldn't say it nicely
Cannot say precisely   Why I went astray
              Yes, I'm difficult
But you didn't notice   Did you ever notice
How I longed to be free   I'm just me!

TOGETHER:
Still, love's there, you know
And sun melts the snow
That's how I can go

     Halfway   Halfway

RAKHEL/KALBA SAVUA:
Halfway to home is closer
Than not going home at all

RACHEL: (to MOTHER)
Halfway's a whole lot brighter,
It seems, if you've hit the wall
We could stall...

       (MOTHER joins her.)

> But we'll both feel better
> Moving on

KALBA SAVUA:
> Moving on

RAKHEL:
> Moving on

> KALBA SAVUA/MOTHER
> I'll try to listen
> May not always hear you
> But you needn't fear
> You're not welcome to stay
> Even as you leave me,
> You'll turn around and see

> RAKHEL/RACHEL:
> I know you'll listen
> Still, I will be near you
>
> Stay, I will!
> Even as I leave you,
> You will see

> (all four together)
> The light in my face
> My heart still will race
> We'll run and embrace

> KALBA SAVUA/MOTHER
> Halfway

> RAKHEL/RACHEL:
> Halfway

> (MUSIC under.)

KALBA SAVUA: Well, my child,...

> (Stepping in between RABBI AKIBA and RAKHEL, HE places a hand on AKIBA's shoulder.)

...I didn't choose him, but you found us a fine scholar!

RAKHEL: No, Father. I found a shepherd.

(RAKHEL moves to RABBI AKIBA's other side. SHE pulls AKIBA away, moving in the opposite direction from KALBA SAVUA, as HE stands motionless.
After several steps, AKIBA stops RAKHEL, and with his eyes, "tells" RAKHEL to acknowledge her father. RAKHEL's eyes lock with KALBA SAVUA's. As the MUSIC swells, RAKHEL runs to KALBA SAVUA's waiting arms. After hugging each other strongly but briefly, they let loose, but still holding hands, sing:)

RAKHEL and KALBA SAVUA:
 Halfway

(MUSIC under, quietly. RAKHEL and KALBA SAVUA let go of each other's hands. RAKHEL goes to AKIBA; THEY exit. MEIR exits. KALBA SAVUA exits.)

RACHEL: So, that's it?

RASHI: More to tell, just not now.

RACHEL: You're leaving, too, aren't you?

(RASHI looks over at SHLOMO, who nods as he puts his pencil behind his ear and closes his notebook.)

RASHI: Our job is done.

RACHEL: Thank you.

RASHI: Thank you. Shalom, Mrs. Cohen.

MOTHER: Shalom.

RASHI: Sha—

RACHEL: —Wait! Will I see them again? Will I see you again?

RASHI: You will.

    (The MUSIC under pauses.)
As long as your book is open. Shalom.

SHLOMO: Shalom.

    (MUSIC resumes, as RASHI and SHLOMO disappear. RACHEL and MOTHER eye each other. RACHEL leans her head on her MOTHER'S shoulder. MOTHER strokes RACHEL's hair fondly.)

[End of song. LIGHTS FADE TO BLACK.]

    (MUSIC under: "SO MANY QUESTIONS" theme. The stage is quickly transformed into the "bimah" at RACHEL's synagogue, weeks later. At center, a lectern, behind which RACHEL stands. LIGHTS FADE UP as MUSIC fades down. RABBI LIPPMAN sits off to one side, watching RACHEL with genuine admiration. RACHEL is in the middle of her bat mitzvah speech.)

RACHEL: ...my grandmas and grandpas, for as many hugs as I could ever want; my folks, for a million details, including— and please don't be alarmed when you see it at the entrance to the reception— the camel; and especially Rabbi Lippman, for cheering me on, and yes, I needed a lot of cheering!

You know, a couple of months ago, when I was trying to get ready for today, the Rabbi gave me my Torah portion. Sure, it helped that it was in English, but I still couldn't imagine what Jacob's ladder, or any other five thousand-year-old story, could possibly have to do with my thirteen-year-old life. Then one afternoon, s/he gave me something else— a book of Talmud. And something happened. Something magical. A door to the past had been opened. And when I walked through that door, I met a whole crowd of people who I hope and expect will be my role models and teachers and guides and friends for a long time to come. See, it turns out that some of their stories are an awful lot like mine. I guess history kind of repeats itself. But, you know, much as I treasure all of these new... old... friends.... maybe the most important "new-old" friend I met there was an unexpected traveling companion... and I especially want to thank her today and also congratulate her, because she told me something that makes me just as happy and proud as I hope I've made her. She's decided to study for something she never had when she was my age—her own bat mitzvah! Congratulations, Mom! And thank you for everything! (To the congregation:) And thank you all for coming today!

> (The RABBI and ELAINE COHEN join
> RACHEL on the bimah)

RABBI: Rachel! Beautiful speech!

> (HE gives her a hug.)

RACHEL: (really pleased)
Thank you, Rabbi.

RABBI: (turning to RACHEL's MOTHER)
And Mrs. Cohen! I had no idea...!

MOTHER: Yes, Rabbi, why not?

> (MUSICAL CHORD as the ANCIENTS begin to reappear.)

And I have a lot of friends to help me!

[Song: 'WELCOME TO THE TALMUD! (Reprise)"]

> SOLO MALE ANCIENT:
> Akiba and his sheep
>
> SOLO FEMALE ANCIENT:
> And Jacob fast asleep
>
> BOTH:
> The Talmud helps them leap
> Across a thousand years
>
> RABBI AKIBA, RAKHEL:
> From centuries before
>
> Add MEIR, ROMAN SOLDIER, FEMALE ANCIENT:
> They're standing at the door
>
> Add MOTHER, STUART, SARAH, RABBI:
> Excited to the core
> To meet their modern peers
>
> ALL:
> Now all of you can take your place
> With Rachels, old and new
> Singing with the joy
> Of what it means to be a Jew

RACHEL: I'm so psyched — my family and all my old friends are getting to meet my..

RACHEL/MOTHER: (laughing) .....really old friends!

ALL:
    So, welcome to the Talmud
    Welcome to our choir
    We come to enlighten, inform and inspire
    Welcome to the Talmud
    It's a magical tome
    Oh welcome, and please
    Consider it home!

RACHEL: Welcome, and please
        Consider it home!

ENSEMBLE:
    Ooh, ooh
    Ah, ah

        (A final tableau is struck, the ANCIENTS
        encircling the MODERNS, with
        RACHEL and her MOTHER in the
        center of them all.)

        [END OF PLAY]

CURTAIN CALL :

(Company bows, followed by:)

[Song: "ANYONE CAN! (Finale)]

ALL:
Why should the Torah
Be kept from the average man?
Who gains from Torah?
Anyone can!

Why should God's teachings
Be claimed by a privileged clan?
Who can best learn from them?
Anyone can!

MALES: If you open wide the book

FEMALES: You'll find us there inviting

MALES: Saying: "Come and take a look!"

FEMALES: You may decide to stay

ALL: Are we strangers when we meet?
Or are we reuniting?
Delighting that we have found our way!

Torah and Talmud
Two halves of a marvelous plan
Come and be part
Never too late to start it

RACHEL: And anyone,

RACHEL/MOTHER: (smiling at each other)
Anyone can!

ALL: Anyone, anyone can!

(BLACKOUT)

About the Authors

Judith Z. Abrams (dramaturgy) was ordained at Hebrew Union College in 1985. She earned her Ph.D. in Rabbinic literature from the Baltimore Hebrew University in 1993.

Rabbi Abrams is the founder and director of Maqom: A School for Adult Talmud Study, online, (*http://www.maqom.com*), where everyone, regardless of background, can come and learn.

She received the Covenant Award for outstanding performance in the field of Jewish Education. She teaches through the ALEPH rabbinic program and is the author of many books about Talmud and prayer.

Rabbi Abrams is available to speak and teach throughout the country, as she has done for many years.

She can be reached at Maqom, POB 31900-323, Houston, TX 77231, (713) 723-2918, email: maqom@compassnet.com.

David Schechter (book and lyrics) has written and directed many contributions to the Jewish theatre genre including his award winning Off Broadway play, "Hannah Senesh"; his highly acclaimed adaptations of Isaac Bashevis Singer's "Gimpel the Fool" and "From the Diary of One Not Born"; "Guarding the Garden", excerpted in the "Torah of the Earth" series and *Lilith Magazine*; "Double Crossed: The Saga of the St. Louis" commissioned by the U. S. Holocaust Museum in Washington, DC; "Shlomo" a musical based on the life and music of Rabbi Shlomo Carlebach. He won an international screenwriting award for his feature film, "Interview", directed by Steve Buscemi and also co-wrote "Blind Date" directed by Stanley Tucci. He lives in NYC where he is currently at work on "Seen", a mystical theatrical collaboration with his beloved partner, Bill Von Hoene. He may be reached at InsideJobSite@aol.com.

Ned Paul Ginsburg (book, music and additional lyrics) has earned composing honors from The National Endowment for the Arts, The National Academy of Recording Arts & Sciences, The International Association of Jazz Educators, The Songwriters Guild of America, and *Downbeat* magazine. Commissioned theater pieces as composer and co-bookwriter include "They Chose Me" and "Fashion Statement" for TADA! and "Arnie!, The TV Musical" for Silver Burdett Ginn. He has also written songs and scores for television, film and educational print, including The Disney Channel, Nederlander TV, ABC-TV, CBS-TV, Warner Bros. Publications, and Scott Foresman.

Additionally, Ned has been a contributing orchestrator to "Beauty And The Beast" (on Broadway), "Minnelli On Minnelli", "Wonder Pets", "Paper Moon", "Casper—The Musical", "The Academy Awards Show", "Radio City Easter Show", "Night Of 1000 Stars", "New York Pops At Carnegie", "Inside Out", and to several Warner Bros. films, included the Oscar-nominated *Michael Collins*. He has worked for or with such composers as Alan Menken, Elliot Goldenthal, Bobby Lopez, Michael-John LaChiusa, Larry Grossman, Jerry Bock, and Jason Robert Brown, and for the entertainers Bernadette Peters, Diahann Carroll, Liza Minnelli, Elaine Stritch, Chita Rivera, Kathie Lee Gifford, Tony Danza, Faith Prince, and many, many others. From 1993-2000 he produced and arranged the highly acclaimed cd series "The Broadway Kids", showcasing young performers singing classic and modern musical theater songs.

Also from Ben Yehuda Press

Torah & Company

The weekly portion of Torah, accompanied by generous helpings of Mishnah and Gemara, served up with discussion questions to spice up your Sabbath table.

Judith Z. Abrams

This useful book offers brief excerpts from each Torah portion, along with appropriately related selections from the Mishnah and Gemara—the Talmud. Discussion questions for each selection are provided to spark open-ended conversation around dinner tables, and wherever else Jews gather to learn and argue.

The texts are short and provocative—the questions even more so. This book promises lively debate, where the deepest text of all is your learning partner.

A great way to learn more Torah, and more about the people you care about most!

978-0-9769862-1-8 / Trade Paperback, 6 x 9, 132 pp. / $12.95

Turn the page for an excerpt from Torah & Company.

Bereishit

BEGINNINGS

Genesis 1:1

In a beginning, God created the heavens and the earth.

Mishnah Hagigah 2:1

The Work of Creation may not be taught to more than one student at a time.... Whoever contemplates these four questions, it would have been better for him not to have come into the world: What is above the world? What is below? What is before? What is after?

Bavli Eruvin 13b

For three years, there was a dispute between the School of Shammai and the School of Hillel, the former claiming: The law is in agreement with our views. And the latter claiming: The law is in agreement with our views.

Then a voice came out of heaven and said: Both of these views are the words of the living God, but the law goes according to the School of Hillel's rulings.

But if both are the words of the living God, why is the law set according to the School of Hillel? Because they behaved modestly and like *mentshes**. They studied Shammai's rules as well as their own and even mentioned Shammai's words before they said their own.

---

* Yiddish for "gentlemen"

Discussion Questions

1. The first word of the Torah, *bereishit,* is generally translated "In *the* beginning". Strictly speaking, however, it means "In *a* beginning". How does this change your understanding of this verse?

2. Do you agree with the Mishnah's assertion that questioning the mechanics of Creation is an invasion of God's privacy? Does God have some secrets that shouldn't be explored? Do you feel entitled to your secrets? Does having secrets put distance between you and your loved ones? Does keeping secrets sometimes allow you to be closer to them?

3. For the Bavli, the voice of God which in the beginning created the world now speaks through the disparate voices of the schools of Shammai and Hillel.

It appears, then, that God speaks in many voices and that there may be many correct answers. This idea should lead to tolerance and humility. Do you think you could practice this intellectual discipline in your own life — thinking that God's truth is everywhere and that success goes to those who act in a mannerly fashion?

*Look for more tales of
Rabbi Akiba
and his colleagues in*

Yonah Lavery's
Talmud Illuminated (Berachot)

available now at
http://talmudcomics.net
and coming soon from Ben Yehuda Press

Torah / Tanakh / Bible

Torah Journeys: The Inner Path to the Promised Land
by *Rabbi Shefa Gold*
The Torah becomes a path of personal, spiritual growth in this first guide to the weekly Torah portion from a Jewish Renewal perspective.
Quality PB, 238 pp. ISBN 978-0-9769862-6-3, $19.95

In the Fever of Love: An Illumination of the Song of Songs
by *Rabbi Shefa Gold*
A poetic response to the Song of Songs, moving from the Biblical verses to a deeply personal, highly erotic meditation on the love of God.
Quality PB, 112 pp. ISBN 978-1-934730-26-3 $14.95   HC, ISBN 978-1-934730-25-6 $27.50

The Yeshivat Chovevei Torah Tanakh Companion to the Book of Samuel
Bible study in the spirit of open and moden orthodoxy
Thirteen eye-opening close readings of the Book of Samuel offer new perspectives on familiar stories while always remaining true to the text.
Quality PB, 268 pp. ISBN 978-0-9769862-4-9 $19.95

Wrestling with Jacob
Deception, Identity, and Freudian Slips in Genesis
Close literary and psychological readings of the Biblical text.
by *Shmuel Klitsner*
Quality PB, 186 pp. ISBN 9781934730-16-4 $17.95

Jewish Thought

Ahron's Heart: The Prayers, Teachings and Letters of Ahrele Roth, A Hasidic Reformer
by *Rabbi Hillel Goelman* and *Rabbi Zalman Schachter Shalomi*
The writings of one of the 20th century's most important Hasidic thinkers.
Quality PB, 160 pp. ISBN 978-1-934730-18-8 $14.95

The Essential Writings of Abraham Isaac Kook
by *Ben Zion Bokser*
The chief rabbi at his spiritual best in an accessible anthology highlighting his most universal teachings.
Quality PB, 220 pp. ISBN 978-0-9769862-3-2 $19.95

Available from BenYehudaPress.com, Amazon.com and BN.com

Talmud

The Hillel Narratives: *What the Tales of the First Rabbi Can Teach Us About Our Judaism*
by *Louis Rieser* Foreword by *Judith Z. Abrams*
"Louis Rieser has reopened the Rabbinic stories and made them interesting again." —Jacob Neusner
Quality PB, 160 pp. ISBN 978-1-934730-22-5 $17.95

Fiction

The Cabalist's Daughter
by *Yori Yanover*
The cloned offspring of the Grand Rabbi and would-be-messiah turns out a girl in this comic, cosmic thriller with a mystical twist.
Quality PB, 280 pp. ISBN 978-0-9789980-9-7 $18.95

A Delightful Compendium of Consolation
by *Burton L. Visotzky*
The Arabian Nights meets the Cairo Geniza in this coming-of-age tale set against the rise of Jewish fortune and influence under Muslim rule.
Quality PB, 328 pp. ISBN 978-1-934730-20-1 $18.95

The Lilac Tree
by *Nicolette Maleckar*
An enchanting tale of love and adventure in the rubble of post-war Berlin.
Quality PB, 188 pp. ISBN 978-0-9769862-2-5 $17.50

Poetry

From The Coffee House of Jewish Dreamers
by *Isidore Century*
Two sides of the poet declared "wonderful" by the *New York Jewish Week*. "Parsha Poems" provides a double-take on the weekly Torah portion; "Tales of Wonder and Wandering" describe the poet's journeys of the body and the soul.
Quality PB, 200 pp. ISBN 978-0-9769862-8-7 $14.95

Available from BenYehudaPress.com, Amazon.com and BN.com

www.ingramcontent.com/pod-product-compliance
Lightning Source LLC
LaVergne TN
LVHW051835080426
835512LV00018B/2889